THE
DOG LOVER'S GUIDE
TO LAKE TAHOE

THE
DOG LOVER'S GUIDE
TO LAKE TAHOE

by Susie Denison

TIMBERCREEK PUBLISHING

Timbercreek Publishing
PO Box 1547
Carnelian Bay, CA 96140
E-Mail Address: sd.timbercreekpub@usa.net

To order books, please call Timbercreek Publishing at (530) 546-0618.

Notice

This is intended as a guide to provide information and is not an
endorsement or recommendation by the author. No liability is
assumed, with respect to the accuracy and completeness of the information or from any loss or injury incurred from the use of this book.
All maps used in this book are for reference only, they are not guar-
anteed to be accurate. Mileages used in this book may vary.

Cover Photo: Susie Denison
Back Cover Photo: Ben Farber
All Other Photos: Susie Denison
Cover Design: Lake Lizard Graphix
Maps: Lake Lizard Graphix

ISBN: 0-9664908-0-0
Library of Congress Catalog
Card Number: 98-96270

Printed in the United States of America.

DEDICATION

This book is dedicated to Ben for being my inspiration. To Mom and Dad for introducing me to dogs. And to Buddy, Zoey and Tucker for always putting a smile on my face.

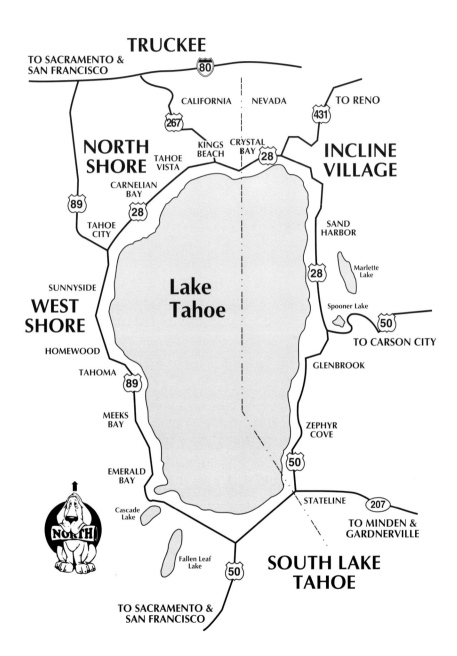

Table of Contents

Lodging
Truckee 12
North Shore 12
West Shore 14
Incline Village 15
South Lake Tahoe 15

Campgrounds
Truckee 22
North Shore 23
West Shore 24
Incline Village 25
South Lake Tahoe 25

Restaurants
Truckee 30
North Shore 31
West Shore 34
Incline Village 35
South Lake Tahoe 36

Hiking Trails
Truckee 42
North Shore. 44
West Shore. 45
Incline Village 48
South Lake Tahoe 49

Mountain Biking Trails
Truckee 56
North Shore. 58
West Shore. 59
Incline Village 60
South Lake Tahoe 61

Cross Country Skiing
Truckee 64
North Shore. 65
West Shore. 65
Incline Village 66
South Lake Tahoe 67

Sledding Hills

Truckee 70
North Shore 70
Incline Village 70
South Lake Tahoe 71

Swimming Areas

Truckee 74
North Shore 74
West Shore 75
Incline Village 75
South Lake Tahoe 76

Fishing Spots

Truckee 80
West Shore 81
Incline Village 82
South Lake Tahoe 82

Other Doggie Adventures

Truckee 86
North Shore 86
West Shore 89
Incline Village 89
South Lake Tahoe 90

Dog Services

Pet Shops 94
Veterinarians 95
Dog Groomers 97
Dog Kennels 98
Dog Sitters 100
Dog Trainers 102
Dog Fencing 103

Lake Tahoe Dog Laws 104
Sno-Park Permits 104
Wilderness Permits 105
Tahoe Dog Tips 106
Maps of Lake Tahoe 108
A Word About Dogs 114
Index 121

Important Phone Numbers

Animal Shelters
- Truckee Animal Shelter (530) 582-7830
- Placer County Animal Shelter (530) 546-4269
- El Dorado County Animal Shelter, SLK Tahoe (530) 577-1766
- Wildlife Rescue, North Lake Tahoe (530) 546-1211
- Lake Tahoe Wildlife Care, SLK Tahoe (530) 577-2273
- Pet Network of North Lake Tahoe (702) 832-4404
- Humane Society of Truckee (530) 587-5948
- South Lake Tahoe Humane Society (530) 577-4521

Emergency Numbers
- Animal Poison Control (800) 548-2423
- Donner-Truckee Vet Emergency Services (530) 587-4366
- North Lake Vet Emergency Services (530) 583-8587
- Incline Vet Emergency Services (702) 831-0433
- South Tahoe Vet Emergency Services (530) 541-3551

Talkline Free Pet Care Tips
Dial 541-0200 or 546-7251, then enter a 4 digit code:

9522	Dental Care	9533	Exercise
9523	Distemper	9534	Feeding & Nutrition
9524	Eye & Ear Care	9535	Grooming
9525	First Aid	9536	Housebreaking
9526	Fleas	9537	Older Dogs
9527	Parvovirus	9538	Puppy Care
9528	Rabies	9539	Shots
9529	Skin Problems	9540	Spaying & Neutering
9530	When to Call the Vet	9541	Training
9531	Worms	9542	Traveling
9532	Choosing a Dog		

A dog is not 'almost human' and I know of no greater insult to the canine race than to describe it as such.

–John Holmes

LODGING

Bernie, St. Bernard Mix

Truckee

Alpine Village Motel
Walk to Donner Lake. Rates are $45 to $70 a night, dogs stay free. 11260 Deer Field Drive, Truckee (530) 587-1787 or (800) 933-1787

Super 8 Lodge
One dog per room. Hot tub, sauna, free continental breakfast. Rates are $63 to $105 a night, and $11 per dog per night. 11506 Deer Field Drive, Truckee (530) 587-8888

Sunset Inn
Located in downtown Truckee near the high school. Rates are $45 to $55 a night, dogs stay free. 11700 Donner Pass Road, Truckee (530) 587-8234

North Shore

Coldwell Banker Hauserman Rentals
Coldwell Banker's rental office has cabins and houses for you and your dog to stay in. No more having to worry about where to leave your dog when you go skiing. Choose from rustic cabins to lakefront homes. The rentals that allow dogs go quickly, so make your reservations early. Check out their web site, where you can find pictures, rates and descriptions of all their vacation homes (www.2ctahoe.com). Rates are $65 to $400 a night, with a $15 extra cleaning fee for dogs. 475 North Lake Blvd, Tahoe City (530) 583-3793 or (800) 20-TAHOE

Holiday House
These lakefront rooms share a large deck with a panoramic view of Lake Tahoe. BBQ, hot tub, and boat buoy available. Rates are $85 to $125 a night, with a $25 dog fee. 7276 North Lake Blvd, Tahoe Vista (530) 546-2369

Rustic Cottages

Previously Tatami Cottage Resort, these cozy cabins have all been upgraded. Complimentary continental breakfast and free video rental. Rates are $49 to $139 a night, and $10 per dog per night. 7499 North Lake Blvd, Tahoe Vista (530) 546-3523

North Shore Lodge

Your choice of a cabin or a room. There is a fenced in BBQ area to let your dog run. Swimming pool open during summer. Rates are $50 to $145 a night, and $5 per dog per night. 8755 North Lake Blvd, Kings Beach (530) 546-4833

Woodvista Lodge

Hot tub open all year, pool open in summer. Rates are $45 to $90 a night, and $10 per dog per night. 7699 North Lake Blvd, Tahoe Vista (530) 546-3839

Stevenson's Inn

Just follow the path to the lake! Hot tub and swimming pool open during summer. No leaving pets alone in your room. More than one dog welcome. Rates are $50 to $105 a night, and $5 per dog per night. 8742 North Lake Blvd, Kings Beach (530) 546-2269 or (800) 634-9141

The Falcon Lodge

Lakefront rooms available. Private sandy beach that allows dogs. Indoor spa and large heated swimming pool open in summer. Rates are $40 to $129 a night, and $10 per dog per night. 8258 North Lake Blvd, Kings Beach (530) 546-2583

Family Tree Restaurant & Motel

Located right in Tahoe City. Walking distance to stores, restaurants and movies. Rates are $40 to $80 a night, dogs stay free. 551 North Lake Blvd, Tahoe City (530) 583-0287

Maya, Husky Pup

North Lake Lodge
Choose from a room or private cabin, some with kitchens. Hot tub, walk to the lake. Rates are $55 to $80, and $5 per dog per night. 8716 North Lake Blvd, Kings Beach (530) 546- 2731

West Shore

Tahoma Lodge
These cabins have a full kitchen and a woodstove or fireplace. Pool, jacuzzi and access to a private beach. Rates are $45 to $115 a night, dogs stay free. 7018 West Lake Blvd, Tahoma (530) 525-7721

Norfolk Woods Inn
These cozy cabins have 2 bedrooms upstairs and a full kitchen downstairs. Rates are $130 to $150 a night, plus a $10 dog fee. 6941 West Lake Blvd, Tahoma (530) 525-5000

Tahoe Lake Cottages
Your choice of a 1 or 2 bedroom cabin with a full kitchen. Pool, jacuzzi and BBQ area. Rates are $125 to $185 a night, dogs stay free. 7030 West Lake Blvd, Tahoma (530) 525-4411

Homeside Motel
Walking distance to the Homewood Ski Resort and the lake. Rates are $55 to $85 a night, dogs stay free. 5205 West Lake Blvd, Homewood (530) 525-9990

Incline Village

Coldwell Banker Incline Realty Inc.
Stay in a house or a condo. There are only a few that allow dogs, so make your reservations early. Rates are $85 to $225 a night. 795 Mays Blvd, Incline Village (702) 831-4800 or (800) 572-5009

South Lake Tahoe

Lake Tahoe Accommodations
Choose from a wide selection of rental homes, mostly located near Heavenly Valley. Rates are $88 to $145 a night. 2048 Dunlap Drive, SLK Tahoe (530) 544-3234 or (800) 544-3234

Lake Tahoe Lodging
There are a few rental homes that allow dogs, so make your reservations early. Rates are $ 125 to $325 a night. 292 Kingsbury Grade, Stateline (702) 588-5253 or (800) 654-5253

Harrah's Tahoe
Dogs are not allowed in the rooms, but Rover can stay in one of Harrah's 5 kennels, free of charge! There are grassy areas outside, and the beach is just a 10 minute walk. Along with a swimming pool and 2 hot tubs, Harrah's has a health club and 6 restaurants. Rates are $99 to $200 a night. Hwy 50, Stateline (702) 588-6611 or (800) 427-7247

Alder Inn
Close to Heavenly Ski Resort. Swimming pool and hot tub. Rates are $39 to $105 a night, and $5 per dog per night with a $10 minimum. 1072 Ski Run Bl, SLK Tahoe (530) 544-4485

Tahoe Country Inn
Rooms available that sleep 6 -10 people with fenced yards for your dog. Rates are $30 to $200 a night, dogs stay free. 4085 Pine Bl, SLK Tahoe (530) 544-5015

Ravenwood Hotel
There are limited rooms that allow dogs. All rooms have gas fireplaces, microwaves and refrigerators. Swimming pool and hot tub. Rates are $42 to $79 a night, with a $10 dog fee. 4075 Manzanita Ave, SLK Tahoe (800) 659-4185

Blue Jay Lodge
Some of these rooms have fireplaces and kitchens. Swimming pool and hot tub. Rates are $39 to $99, and $10 per dog per night. 4133 Cedar Ave, SLK Tahoe (800) 258-3529

High Country Lodge
This rustic lodge is located near Emerald Bay. Hot tub. Rates are $30 to $125 a night, with a $5 dog fee. 1227 Emerald Bay Road, SLK Tahoe (530) 541-0508

La Baer Inn
These recently remodeled rooms are located right across from the casinos. Rates are $30 to $100 a night, with a refundable $10 deposit for dogs. 4133 Lake Tahoe Bl, SLK Tahoe (530) 544-2139

Lakepark Lodge
There are limited rooms that allow dogs. Located 1 block from casinos and 2 blocks from the lake. Hot Tub. Rates are $40 to $70 a night, with a $10 fee and a $40 refundable deposit for dogs. 4081 Cedar Ave, SLK Tahoe (530) 541-5004

The Montgomery Inn

These quiet rooms are only 2 blocks from the lake. Hot tub. Rates are $35 to $98 a night, and $5 per dog per night. 966 Modesto Ave, SLK Tahoe (530) 544-3871

Tahoe Marina Inn

Small dogs are allowed October through May only, and not on holidays. Private beach, swimming pool. Rates are $60 to $129 a night, dogs stay free. 930 Bal Bijou Rd, SLK Tahoe (530) 541-2180

Blue Lake Motel

Walk to the marina and restaurants from this cozy motel. Swimming pool and hot tub. Rates are $40 to $70 a night, and $10 per dog per night. 1055 Ski Run Bl, SLK Tahoe (530) 541-2399

Toby, Golden Retriever

Tahoe Valley Motel
There are limited rooms that allow dogs. All rooms have gas fireplaces. Dogs may not be left in rooms alone. Swimming pool, hot tub. Rates are $95 to $125 a night, $5 per dog per night. 2241 Lake Tahoe Bl, SLK Tahoe (530) 541-0353

Manzanita Motel
This motel is located by National Forest, near Camp Richardson and Emerald Bay. Rates are $35 to $50 a night, dogs stay free. 532 Emerald Bay Rd, SLK Tahoe (530) 541-5059

Trade Winds Motel
There are limited rooms that allow dogs. Laundry facilities, swimming pool, hot tub. Private beach that allows dogs. Walk to casinos. Rates are $35 to $125 a night, $5 per dog per night, and a $50 deposit. 944 Friday Ave, SLK Tahoe (530) 544-6459

Best Western Lake Tahoe Inn
These rooms are located 1/2 block from the casinos. Complimentary breakfast. Swimming pool and hot tub. Rates are $49 to $104 a night. Dogs require a $100 deposit. 4110 Lake Tahoe Bl, SLK Tahoe (530) 541-2010

Red Carpet Inn
This inn is located 1/2 block from the casinos. Swimming pool and hot tub. Complimentary donuts and coffee for breakfast. Rates are $49 to $110 a night, dogs stay free. 4100 Lake Tahoe Bl, SLK Tahoe, (530) 544-2261

Motel 6
One small dog per room allowed. Swimming pool. Rates are $33 to $43 a night, dogs stay free. 2375 Lake Tahoe Bl, SLK Tahoe (530) 542-1400 or (800) 440-6000

Timberlake Inn

There is a grass area for your dog to play. Located 300 yards from the lake. Rates are $30 to $85 a night, with a $5 dog fee. 993 San Jose Ave, SLK Tahoe (530) 544-3586

Beachside Inn & Suite

Walk to the beach, casinos, and restaurants. Sauna and spa. Rates are $30 to $110 a night, and $5 per dog per night. 930 Park Ave, SLK Tahoe (800) 884-4920

Days Inn- Stateline South Lake Tahoe

There are limited rooms that allow dogs. Dogs may not be left alone in room late at night or early in the morning. Dogs are not allowed over holidays. Rates are $42 to $108 a night, and $5 per dog per night. 3 dog maximum per room. 968 Park Ave, SLK Tahoe (530) 541-4800 or (800) 325-2525

No matter how little money and how few possessions you own,
having a dog makes you rich.

–Louis Sabin

CAMPGROUNDS

Coco, Chocolate Lab

Truckee

Donner Memorial State Park

This campsite offers many recreational activities, including fishing, swimming, rafting, canoeing, hiking, nature walks, and watercraft rentals. There is a lagoon and Donner Lake to explore. Dogs must be leashed. Closed for the winter. 154 sites, $12 to $16 fee and $1 per dog per day. From Truckee, drive west 3 miles on Donner Pass Road. For more information, call (800) 444-PARK.

Cottonwood Campground

Located along Cottonwood Creek, this private campsite is fairly secluded from the highway. Enjoy fishing and hiking. Dogs must be leashed. Closed for the winter. 49 sites, $9 fee. From Truckee, drive north on Hwy 89 for 19.5 miles . Look for the sign on the side of the highway. For more information, call (800) 280-CAMP.

Logger Campground

This large, well maintained campsite has paved roads and a nearby public boat ramp. Enjoy fishing and boating on the Stampede Reservoir. Dogs must be leashed. Closed for the winter. 252 sites, $11 fee. From Truckee, drive 7 miles east on I- 80 and take the Hirschdale Exit. Turn on the Boca-Stampede Road, and drive north for 8 miles to the campsite. For more information, call
(800) 280-CAMP.

Martis Creek Campground

This secluded campground is well maintained and has private, well-spaced sites. There is hiking, mountain biking, and fly fishing nearby. The campground is located near the Truckee-Tahoe Airport, so there may be some noise. Dogs must be leashed. Closed for the winter. 25 sites, $10 fee. From Truckee, drive south on Hwy 267 for 5 miles and turn left at the Martis Creek sign. For more information, call (530) 639-2342.

Granite Flat Campground

Located just south of Truckee, on Hwy 89, this riverfront campground is a great spot for fishing. Dog must be leashed. Closed for the winter. 72 sites, $12 fee. Located 3/4 of a mile south of Truckee on Hwy 89. For more information, call (800) 280-CAMP.

North Shore

Goose Meadows Campground

This campsite is right on the Truckee River. It is also right on Hwy 89. There is traffic noise, and not much privacy. But the fishing is great! Dogs must be leashed. Closed for the winter. 27 sites, $8 fee. Located approximately 9 miles north of Tahoe City on Hwy 89. For more information, call (800) 280-CAMP.

Silver Creek Campground

Located on the Truckee River, this campsite is very close to Hwy 89. You and your dog can hike up Deer Creek, or fish in the Truckee River. This campground is just south of Goose Meadows. Dogs must be leashed. Closed for the winter. 31 sites, $8 fee. Located approximately 6 miles north of Tahoe City on Hwy 89, near Squaw Valley. For more information, call (800) 280-CAMP.

Tahoe State Recreation Area

This lakefront campground is right in Tahoe City. It's in walking distance to shops, restaurants and is right next to the bike path. It's also right on the main road, so it may be noisy. Dogs must be leashed. Closed for the winter. 31 sites, $16 fee, dogs are $1 a day. Located just east of the Safeway Shopping Center in Tahoe City. For more information, call (800) 444-PARK.

Sandy Beach Campground

Located in Tahoe Vista, this campsite has easy access to the lake. Dogs must be leashed. Closed for the winter. 44 sites, $15 to $20 fee. Located at 6873 North Lake Blvd, Tahoe Vista. For more information, call (530) 546-7682.

Lake Forest Campground

This campground, located just outside Tahoe City, has a boat ramp, a pier, and a small rocky beach for your dog to swim. Dogs must be leashed. Closed for the winter. 20 sites, $12 fee. From Tahoe City, drive east on Hwy 28 for 2 miles. Turn right on Lake Forest Road, and right into the campground. For more information, call (530) 583-5544.

West Shore

William Kent Campground

Situated close to the lake, bike path, and Sunnyside Lodge, this campsite has plenty to keep you busy. Dogs must be leashed. Closed for the winter. 95 sites, $12 fee. From Tahoe City, drive 2 miles south on Hwy 89. For more information, call (800) 280-CAMP.

Kaspian Campground

This small campsite is in Blackwood Canyon and is close to the lake and bike path. There can be highway noise. Dogs must be leashed. Closed for the winter. 10 sites, $10 fee. From Tahoe City, drive 5 miles south on Hwy 89. For more information, call (800) 280-CAMP.

General Creek Campground

One of just a few campsites open over winter. Located at Sugar Pine Point State Park and near the lake, bike path and hiking trails. Dogs must be leashed and are only allowed in the campground and on paved roads. Open all year. 175 sites, $16 fee. From Tahoe City, drive south 9 miles on Hwy 89 to General Creek Campground and Sugar Pine Point State Park. For more information, call (800) 444-PARK.

Meeks Bay Campground

Located close to Hwy 89, this campsite has little privacy and can be noisy. It does, however have a private sandy beach and boat ramp. Dogs must be leashed. Closed for the winter. 40 sites, $14 fee. For more information, call (800) 280-CAMP.

Incline Village

Mount Rose Campground

This campsite is in the Toiyabe National Forest, and is surrounded by great hiking trails. Dogs must be leashed. Closed for the winter. 24 sites, $8 fee. Drive north on Hwy 431 (Mount Rose Hwy) for 9 miles. The campsite is on your right. For more information, call (800) 280-CAMP.

South Lake Tahoe

Emerald Bay State Park

Secluded from the highway, this large campground has wonderful views of the lake. There is a 1/4 mile hike to the Emerald Bay Beach from most sites. This is a very popular spot. Dogs must be leashed, and are only allowed in the campground and on paved roads. Closed for the winter. 100 sites, $16 fee. For more information, call (800) 444-PARK.

Emerald Bay Boat-In Camp

One of the most popular campsites around, this spot is complete with a large pier and a long sandy beach. Check out Vikingsholm during the day, and camp here at night. Dogs must be leashed and are not allowed in Vikingsholm. Closed for the winter. 20 sites, $10 fee. Located on the north side of Emerald Bay. For more information, call (530) 525-7277.

Fallen Leaf Lake Campground

This private and secluded campsite offers swimming, hiking, fishing, biking and boating. Dogs must be leashed. Closed for the winter. 205 sites, $14 fee. From South Lake Tahoe Y, drive 2 miles north on Hwy 89 to Fallen Leaf Lake Road. For more information, call (800) 280-CAMP.

South Lake Tahoe Recreation Area

Located just off Hwy 50, this campsite is nicely maintained and offers access to a nearby pool and fitness center. Enjoy swimming and boating in the lake. This is a great spot for RVs. Dogs must be leashed. Closed for the winter. 160 sites, $16.50 fee, plus $1 per dog per day. From South Lake Tahoe Y, drive east on Hwy 50 for 2.5 miles to Rufus Allen Blvd. Follow the signs to the campsite. For more information, call (530) 542-6096.

Tahoe Valley Campground

Just off the main road, this large, clean campsite is a great family spot. Enjoy a swimming pool, tennis courts and the Upper Truckee River, which runs through the campsite. Dogs must be leashed. Closed for the winter. 412 sites, $20 to $29 fee. From South Lake Tahoe Y, drive south on Hwy 50 for 1/2 mile. Turn left on C St. and follow the signs to the campsite. For more information, call (530) 541-2222.

KOA of South Lake Tahoe

This campsite right off Hwy 50 has a swimming pool, a small market, and is near the Upper Truckee River. Dogs must be leashed. Closed for the winter. 60 sites, $23 to $29 fee. Dogs are an extra $3.50 per dog per day. From South Lake Tahoe Y, drive south on Hwy 50 for 4.6 miles, the campground will be on your left. For more information, call (530) 577-3693.

Tahoe Pines Campground

This campsite is located right next to the KOA Campground. It is right on the Upper Truckee River, and offers a small beach, with places to swim. Dogs must be leashed. Closed for the winter. 80 sites, $22 to $29 fee. Dogs are an extra $3.50 per dog, per day. From South Lake Tahoe Y, drive south on Hwy 50 for 4.5 miles. The campground is on the left. For more information, call (530) 577-1653.

Nevada Beach & Campground

This campsite is next to a sandy beach on the shore of Lake Tahoe. Enjoy swimming, boating, and volleyball. The beach may be packed with people during the day. Dogs must be leashed. Closed for the winter. 54 sites, $16 fee. From South Lake Tahoe, drive east on Hwy 50, 1 mile past Stateline Nevada to Elks Point Road. For more information, call (800) 280-CAMP.

Zephyr Cove Campground

There's not much privacy at this campsite on the beach. This is a very popular beach spot during the day. Enjoy swimming, volleyball and boating. Dogs must be leashed. Open all year. 170 sites, $17 to $24 fee. From South Lake Tahoe, drive northeast on Hwy 50, 14 miles past Stateline Nevada to Zephyr Cove. Follow the signs to the campsite. For more information, call (702) 588-6644.

*There is no psychiatrist in the world
like a puppy licking your face.*

−Bern Williams

RESTAURANTS

Teddy, Springer Spaniel Pup

Truckee

Ames Deli Mart
Deli sandwiches. Sit at an outside table with your dog.
12716 Northwoods, Truckee (530) 587-1717

Dairy Queen
Hamburgers, ice cream. Eat at a table outside, and get a free 'puppy cup' of vanilla ice cream for your dog. 11355 Donner Pass Road, Donner Plaza, Truckee (530) 587-7055

Gateway Deli
Deli sandwiches. Sit with your pooch at an outside table.
11012 Donner Pass Road, Truckee (530) 587-3106

Port of Subs
Sandwiches, salads. Eat at a table outside with your dog.
11260 Donner Pass Road, Truckee (530) 582-8060

Sizzler
Steak, seafood, salad. Your pooch can join you at a picnic table outside. 11262 Donner Pass Road, Truckee (530) 587-1824

Starbucks Coffee
Coffee, bagels, muffins, scones. Have a coffee and a snack with your dog at a table outside. 11260 Donner Pass Road, Truckee
(530) 582-6856

Taco Station
Tacos, burritos. Eat at a table outside with your dog. 10100 West River Road, Truckee (530) 587-8226

Wild Cherries
Sandwiches, soup, salads. Grab a bite to eat at a table outside, and your dog will get a dog biscuit. 11429 Donner Pass Rd, Truckee (530) 582-5602

Zena's
Pancakes, quiche, sandwiches. Dine with your dog at a table outside. 10292 Donner Pass Road, Truckee (530) 587-1771

North Shore

Alpine Cafe
Pizza, deli sandwiches, baked goods. Dine with your dog at a riverside table outside. 150 Alpine Meadows Road, Alpine Meadows (530) 583-6896

The Blue Onion
Gourmet deli sandwiches. Your pooch can join you at an outside table. 7019 North Lake Blvd, Tahoe Vista (530) 546-3915

CB's Pizza & Grill
Pizza, sandwiches, salads. Sit with your dog at an outside table. 5075 North Lake Blvd, Carnelian Bay (530) 546-4738

The Char Pit
Burgers, sandwiches, tacos. Dine on the outside patio with your pooch. 8732 North Lake Blvd, Kings Beach (530) 546-3171

The Coffee Connection
Coffee, bagels, sandwiches. Dogs must be leashed or under the outdoor table. 950 North Lake Blvd, Tahoe City (530) 583-0725

Coyotes Mexican Grill
Tacos, burritos, mexican salads. There's lots of outdoor seating for you and your dog. 521 North Lake Blvd, Tahoe City (530) 583-6653

Fast Eddies Texas Bar-B-Que
Ribs, burgers, sandwiches. Eat at an outside table with your pooch. 690 North Lake Blvd, Tahoe City (530) 583-0950

Fiamma Cucina Rustica
Pizza, pasta, sandwiches. Enjoy this delicious cuisine at one of the outdoor tables. 521 North Lake Blvd, Tahoe City (530) 581-1416

Grazie
Northern Italian Cuisine. Dine with your doggie outside, and enjoy the panoramic lakeviews. 700 North Lake Blvd, Tahoe City (530) 583-0233

Lily Rose, Miniature Schnauzer

The Java Hut

Coffee, pastries, bagel sandwiches. Have a coffee or snack at an outside table with your pooch. 8268 North lake Blvd, Kings Beach (530) 546-0602

Joni's Cafe

Burgers, salads, ice cream. Enjoy your lunch at an outside table with your dog. Open only in the summer. 8421 North Lake Blvd, Kings Beach (530) 546-2715

Kentucky Fried Chicken

Chicken. Eat at a table outside with your pooch. 8697 North Lake Blvd, Kings Beach (530) 546-2715

The Mustard Seed

Vegetarian and health foods. Sit with your doggie at an outside table. 7411 North Lake Blvd, Tahoe Vista (530) 546-3525

Naughty Dawg

Burgers, steaks, sandwiches. Dogs get a bowl of water when they eat with you on the patio. 255 North Lake Blvd, Tahoe City (530) 581-DAWG

Rosie's Cafe

Seafood, ribs, steak. Dine with your doggie at an outdoor table. 561 North Lake Blvd, Tahoe City (530) 583-8504

Subway

Sandwiches, salads. Eat an an outside table with your dog. 8700 North Lake Blvd, Kings Beach (530) 546-8258

Duncan, Black Lab / Dalmation Mix

Syd's Bagelery and Expresso
Coffee, bagel sandwiches. Sit at a table outside with your dog.
550 North Lake Blvd, Tahoe City (530) 583-2666

Wishing Well Espresso & Boutique
Coffee, bagels, muffins. Have a coffee or a snack at a table outside
with your pooch. 8397 North Lake Blvd, Kings Beach (530) 546-9474

West Shore

Izzy's Burger Spa
Burgers, fries, shakes. Share a table outside with your dog, and enjoy
the view of the Truckee River. 100 West Lake Blvd, Tahoe City
(530) 583-4111

Obexer's Country Market
Deli sandwiches. Eat at a picnic table outside with your dog.
5300 West Lake Blvd, Homewood (530) 525-1300

Perkins Pretty Good Kitchen
Gourmet health food. Dine with your doggie at an outside table.
505 West Lake Blvd, Tahoe City (530) 583-3663

Sunnyside Market
Deli and market. Have your lunch at an outside table with your dog.
1780 West Lake Blvd, Sunnyside (530) 583-7626

Tahoe House & Backerei
Homemade soups, sandwiches, baked goods. Dine with your doggie
on the outside patio. 625 West Lake Blvd, Tahoe City
(530) 583-1377

West Shore Cafe
California Cuisine. Dine on the deck with your doggie. Open only in
summer. 5180 West Lake Blvd, Homewood (530) 525-5200

Incline Village

Grog & Grist Market and Deli
Deli sandwiches. Sit with your dog at a table outside. 800 Tahoe Blvd,
Incline Village (702) 831-1123

Hamburger Delite
Burgers, hot dogs, fries. Eat at one of the tables outside with your
dog. 868 Tahoe Blvd, Incline Village (702) 832-2121

T's Mesquite Rotisserie
Sandwiches, burritos, salads. Dine with your doggie at a table outside.
901 Tahoe Blvd, Incline Village (702) 831-2832

Subway
Sandwiches, salads. Sit at a table outside with your dog. 317 Village
Blvd, Incline Village (702) 831-3370

The Wildflower Cafe
Sandwiches, salads. Dine on the patio, while your dog hangs out in the
fenced in area nearby. 869 Tahoe Blvd, Incline Village (702) 831-8072

South Lake Tahoe

Bayer's Bagel Bakery
Bagels, bagel sandwiches. Dine with your doggie at an outdoor table.
2701 Lake Tahoe Blvd, SLK Tahoe (530) 541-7882

Chris' Cafe
Burgers, sandwiches. Sit outside at a table with your dog.
3140 Hwy 50, Meyers (530) 577-5132

Colombo's Burgers A-Go-Go
Burgers, fish & chips, chicken strips. Eat at an outdoor table with
your pooch. 841 Emerald Bay Road, SLK Tahoe (530) 541-4646

Grass Roots Natural Foods
Natural foods. Eat with your dog at an outside table.
2040 Dunlap Drive, SLK Tahoe (530) 541-7788

Izzy's Burger Spa
Burgers, fries, shakes. Share a table outside with your dog.
2591 Hwy 50, SLK Tahoe (530) 544-5030

J&J Pizza
Pizza, calzones, salads. Sit at a table outside with your pooch.
2660 Lake Tahoe Blvd, SLK Tahoe (530) 542-2780

Karp's Pizza
Pizza, calzones, salads. Eat with your dog at an outdoor table.
2297 Lake Tahoe Blvd #2, SLK Tahoe (530) 542-2211

Kentucky Fried Chicken
Chicken. Sit at a table outside with your dog. 2136 Lake Tahoe Blvd,
SLK Tahoe (530) 541-2727

Killer Chicken
Chicken, sandwiches. Leashed dogs can eat with you at an outside
table. 2660 Hwy 50, SLK Tahoe (530) 542-9977

Meyers Downtown Cafe
Breakfast, lunch. Eat at a table outside with your dog. 3200 Hwy 50,
Meyers (530) 573-0228

Axel Rod, German Shepherd

Rude Brothers Bagel & Coffee Haus
Coffee, bagels, cookies, cinnamon rolls. Have a coffee or a snack at a table outside with your dog. 3117 Harrison Ave, SLK Tahoe (530) 541-8195

Scott's Delicatessen
Deli sandwiches. Sit at a table outside with your dog. Elk Point Road & Hwy 50, Zephyr Cove (702) 588-7303

Sidestreet Cafe
Bagels, sandwiches, baked goods. Dine with your doggie at a table outside. 3988 Lake Tahoe Blvd, SLK Tahoe (530) 544-5393

Sierra Deli & Market
Deli sandwiches. Eat with your pooch at a table outside and your dog will get a treat. 3141 Emerald Bay Road, SLK Tahoe (530) 577-3068

Snow Flake Drive In
Burgers, fries. Sit at a table outside with your dog. 3057 Lake Tahoe Blvd, SLK Tahoe (530) 544-6377

South Shore Cafe
Sandwiches, burgers. Eat at an outside table with your pooch. 292 Kingsbury Grade, Stateline (702) 588-7632

Sprouts
Organic health foods, pasta, soup, sandwiches. Dine at a picnic table with your dog. 3125 Harrison Ave, SLK Tahoe (530) 541-6969

Subway
Sandwiches, salads. Eat at a table outside with your dog. 3924 Lake Tahoe Blvd, SLK Tahoe (530) 541-4334

Taco Bell

Tacos, burritos. Sit with your pooch at an outside table.
4109 Lake Tahoe Blvd, SLK Tahoe (530) 541-5233

Tahoe Keys Delicatessen

Deli sandwiches. Dine with your doggie at a table outside.
2301 Hwy 50, SLK Tahoe (530) 544-1335

Ternullo's Creamery & Cafe

Sandwiches, soup, salads. Enjoy your lunch at an outside table with
your dog. 3447 Lake Tahoe Blvd, SLK Tahoe (530) 541-0555

Thirsty Duck Bar & Grill

Friday night, bring your dog to the outside BBQ (ribs and chicken)
during the summer months. Full bar outside. 400 Dorla Ct,
Zephyr Cove (702) 588-3899

Yellow Submarine

Sandwiches, salads. Sit at an outside table with your dog.
Tallac Ave & Hwy 50, SLK Tahoe (530) 541-8808

*If man lived up to the reputation of a dog,
he would be a saint.*

–Zanzibarian Proverb

HIKING TRAILS

Rigel, Siberian Husky

Truckee

Pacific Crest Trail at Donner Pass

8 Miles Roundtrip– Moderate

Hike through lodgepole forests and enjoy beautiful views of Donner Lake. From Truckee, drive 10.5 miles west to the Soda Springs Exit. Turn left and drive past Sugar Bowl to Alpine Skills International. Turn right and drive through the parking lot to the Pacific Crest Trail-head. If you want to shorten this hike, you can hike one way and come out at the Pacific Crest Trail, at the Castle Peak Exit off I-80.

Donner Peak

3.5 Miles Roundtrip– Easy

Bring a picnic and enjoy the expansive views of Donner Lake and Lake Tahoe. From Truckee, drive west on the I-80 for 10.5 miles to the Soda Springs Exit. Turn left and drive past Sugar Bowl to Alpine Skills International. Turn right and drive through the parking lot to the Pacific Crest Trailhead. After parking, begin your hike at the Overland Emigrant Trail. Turn left at the Mount Judah Loop junction, and veer left at the Emigrant Wagon Trail. Continue to Emigrant Pass, turn left and hike up hill to Donner Peak.

Mt. Lola

9 Miles Roundtrip– Strenuous

This hike will take you through willow groves, open meadows, across creeks and ponds, and you will end up at 9,148 feet elevation with breathtaking panoramic vistas. From Truckee, head north on Hwy 89 for 14.5 miles to Henness Pass Road. Drive west for 1.5 miles to Jackson Meadow. Turn left and go .8 miles toward Independence Lake. After crossing the river, turn right on Old Henness Pass Road. Drive 3.3 miles to the Mt. Lola Trailhead. The trail is marked along the way with white arrows in the dirt and white diamonds on the trees.

Summit Lake

4 Miles Roundtrip– Easy
After passing through a tunnel under the freeway, you will hike through forests and fields of wildflowers. This is a great place to picnic and swim. From Truckee, drive west on I-80 approximately 8 miles and take the Castle Peak Exit. Follow the signs to the Pacific Crest Trailhead and park in the parking lot. Follow the main trail until you see a sign for Summit Lake.

Eagle Lakes

6 Miles Roundtrip– Easy
This is a great spot for fishing, biking and camping. From Truckee, drive west on I-80 for 21 miles to the Eagle Lakes Exit. Go north for .5 miles and make a right on Eagle Lakes Road. Drive on this dirt road to the parking area. Park here and continue up the dirt road to the Eagle Lakes Trailhead.

Loch Leven Lakes Trail

7 Miles Roundtrip– Moderate
This trail will take you over the Southern Pacific Railroad to the first of 3 small lakes. The lakes get warm enough to swim in over summer. This is great spot for fishing and camping. From Truckee, go west on I-80 for 17 miles to the Big Bend Exit. Turn left and drive .6 miles to the parking area across from the Loch Leven Lakes Trailhead.

Frog Point

8.5 Miles Roundtrip– Moderate
Climb through massive granite boulders and meadows of wildflowers and enjoy vistas of Donner Summit. From Truckee, drive west on I-80 for 7.5 miles to the Boreal Ridge Exit, and turn left under the freeway. Make another left and follow the signs to the Pacific Crest Trailhead. Park and begin hiking on the Pacific Crest Trail. Follow this trail until you see signs for Summit Lake/Warren Lake. Follow the signs to Warren Lake and you will begin a climb between Frog Point and Castle Peak. Turn right and continue to Frog Summit.

North Shore

Shirley Lake Trail
5 Miles Roundtrip– Moderate
Watch for stone trail markers, as you climb over large granite boulders. Stay to the left of the creek, and follow it to Shirley Lake. From Tahoe City, drive 5 miles north on Hwy 89 and turn left on Squaw Valley Road. Drive 2.5 miles and turn left toward the Squaw Valley Tram. Turn right on Squaw Peak Road and drive .4 miles to the trailhead.

Squaw Creek Trail
2 Miles Roundtrip– Easy
This trail follows Squaw Creek, past a waterfall and through a meadow filled with wildflowers. From Tahoe City, drive 5 miles north on Hwy 89 and turn left on Squaw Valley Road. Drive 2.2 miles and turn right into Olympic Village. Park past the fire station. The trailhead is at the end of the Olympic Village Inn.

Five Lakes Trail
5 Miles Roundtrip– Moderate
This popular trail climbs for the first 2 miles, then approaches the first of 5 small lakes. There are breathtaking views of Alpine Meadows Ski Area. From Tahoe City, drive approximately 4 miles north on Hwy 89 and turn left on Alpine Meadows Road. Drive 1.5 miles and the trailhead will be on the right, across from Deer Park Drive.

Martis Peak Trail
3.5 Miles Roundtrip– Easy
Enjoy panoramic views of Lake Tahoe from this trail. From Tahoe City, drive east for 9 miles on Hwy 28 and turn left on Hwy 267. Drive north for 3.8 miles and turn left at the dirt turnout and park (.5 miles south of Brockway Summit). Cross Hwy 267 and start up the dirt road. Follow the signs for the Tahoe Rim Trail and veer left at the junction.

Bailey, Beagle

West Shore

Ward Creek Canyon
12 Miles Roundtrip– Moderate
This trail will take you to the top of Twin Peaks with views of Lake Tahoe and the Granite Chief Wilderness. From Tahoe City, drive south on Hwy 89 for 3.2 miles and turn right on Pineland Drive. Turn left on Twin Peaks Road, then follow the signs to Ward Creek Canyon. Drive to the Forest Service Road 15N62 and park. Walk left down the forest service road and follow the signs for Twin Peaks Trail.

Ellis Peak Trail
5 Miles Roundtrip– Moderate
You will hike through forest and meadows, and along the way, see beautiful views of the lake. When the trail splits, go left to Ellis Lake, or right to Ellis Peak. From Tahoe City, drive south on Hwy 89 for 4.2 miles. Turn right on Blackwood Canyon Road, and drive approximately 7 miles until you reach Barker Pass. The trail starts on the south side of the road where the pavement ends.

Eagle Rock
1.5 Miles Roundtrip– Easy
Bring your camera! There are spectacular views from up here. This is a great hike for late afternoon. From Tahoe City, drive south 4.2 miles on Hwy 89 and turn right on Blackwood Canyon Road. The trail begins a quarter mile in on the left. Follow the power lines that climb up a ridge to the south, then veer to the east up Eagle Rock.

Tucker, Golden Retriever Pup

Crag Lake

10 Miles Roundtrip– Moderate
This trail takes you into beautiful Desolation Wilderness. Enjoy the variety of wildflowers in spring. Bring a lunch and eat atop one of the many granite boulders that overlook the lake. A wilderness permit is required for this hike. From Tahoe City, drive south on Hwy 89 for 11 miles to Meeks Bay and park near the Desolation Wilderness Trailhead. Begin your hike down the gated dirt road and veer right at the Tahoe-Yosemite Trail sign. You will pass a small lake, then continue another couple of miles to Crag Lake.

Eagle Falls Trail

3 Miles Roundtrip– Moderate
You will follow a creek and pass a breathtaking waterfall, as you approach Eagle Lake which is surrounded by gigantic granite cliffs. A wilderness permit is required for this hike. From Tahoe City, drive south on Hwy 89 for 18 miles to Emerald Bay. Turn right at the Eagle Falls parking area. Begin your hike at the Eagle Falls Trailhead.

Velma Lakes Trail

11 Miles Roundtrip– Moderate
You will pass beautiful Eagle Lake on your way to Upper, Middle and Lower Velma Lakes. This is a great spot for swimming and camping. A wilderness permit is required for this hike in Desolation Wilderness. From Tahoe City, drive south on Hwy 89 for 18 miles to Emerald Bay. Make a right at the Eagle Falls Trailhead parking lot. Start on the Eagle Falls Trail and veer left at the Velma Lakes Trail sign.

Cascade Falls Trail

2 Miles Roundtrip– Easy
This trail will take you to Cascade Falls overlooking Cascade Lake. Be careful, the rocks can be slippery. Follow the creek upstream and enjoy the large granite boulders and water hole. No wilderness permit required. From Tahoe City, drive south on Hwy 89 for 19 miles to the Bayview Trailhead and Campground. Park and follow the Bay View Trail and veer right at the Cascade Falls Trail.

Granite Lake Trail

2.5 Miles Roundtrip– Moderate

You will enjoy beautiful vistas of Lake Tahoe while hiking up this steep trail. The lake is a great spot for swimming and fishing. A wilderness permit is required for this hike. From Tahoe City, drive south on Hwy 89 for 19 miles to the Bayview Trailhead and Campground. Park and follow the Bayview Trail and veer right at the Cascade Falls Trail. At the next junction go left to Granite Lake.

Incline Village

Skunk Harbor

3 Miles Roundtrip– Moderate

This hike will take you down to the beautiful shoreline of east Lake Tahoe. There is plenty to explore, including The Newhall House, a historic stone house that was built in the 1920's and is now owned by the U.S. Forest Service. This private cove makes a great place for picnicking and swimming. From Tahoe City, drive east on Hwy 28 for 24 miles. Park on the right side of the road, just past Skunk Harbor. Follow the trail down the fire road.

Mount Rose Trail

12 Miles Roundtrip– Moderate

You will hike through fields of wildflowers and along winding creeks. Enjoy spectacular views of Carson City, Lake Tahoe and even Donner Lake. From Incline Village, drive north on Hwy 431 (Mt. Rose Highway) for 7.6 miles to a gated dirt road on the left side of the highway. Park and start your hike up the dirt road. Turn right at the Big Meadow Trail junction to get to the top of Mount Rose.

Ophir Creek Trail

6 Miles Roundtrip– Easy

This trail takes you through Tahoe Meadows, where you can enjoy the wildflowers, and your dog can enjoy the creek that follows along the trail. You will hike through open meadows, thick forests, and rocky canyons and end up at Upper Price Lake. From Incline Village, drive north on Hwy 431 (Mt. Rose Highway) for 6.8 miles. You will see a large open meadow on your right. Park on the side of the road and find the trail by the creek.

South Lake Tahoe

Mount Tallac

10 Miles Roundtrip– Strenuous

You will climb 5 miles and gain over 3,000 feet of elevation to arrive at the top of Mount Tallac, where you will have truly unbelievable views of all of Lake Tahoe. You will pass 2 lakes, which are a great spot for a picnic lunch. Bring a jacket, it can get cold at the top. A wilderness permit is required for this hike. From South Lake Tahoe Y, drive north on Hwy 89 for 3.5 miles. Turn left on the dirt road at the Mount Tallac Trailhead sign across from Baldwin Beach.

The Hawley Grade Trail

3.5 Miles Roundtrip– Easy

This historic hike is on the first wagon road built in the area in the late 1850's. The trails follows the Upper Truckee River. From South Lake Tahoe Y, drive south on Hwy 50 for 5.3 miles and turn left on South Upper Truckee Road. Drive 3.5 miles and turn at the Hawley Grade sign. Continue to the end of the road and park past the houses.

Fallen Leaf Lake Trail

3.5 Miles Roundtrip– Easy

This beautiful lake is a great spot for picnicking, swimming, fishing, and biking. From the South Lake Tahoe Y, drive north on Hwy 89 and turn left on Fallen Leaf Lake Road. Follow the road past the campground to the Fallen Leaf Lake Trailhead.

Susie Lake Trail

8 Miles Roundtrip– Moderate

This scenic trail in Desolation Wilderness passes by creeks and water-falls. Continue another mile past Susie Lake to reach Heather Lake, and another 2 miles to reach Lake Aloha. A wilderness permit is required for this hike. From South Lake Tahoe Y, drive north 3 miles on Hwy 89 and turn left on Fallen Leaf Lake Road. Pass the Fallen Leaf Lodge and continue down the Forest Service Road. Follow the signs toward Lily Lake to the Glen Alpine Trailhead. Park and begin hiking on the gravel road, following the signs to Susie Lake.

Echo Lakes Trail

12 Miles Roundtrip– Moderate

You will begin at Lower Echo Lake and end at Lake Aloha. This is one of the most spectacular hikes in the area! Bring your camera and enjoy the scenery. Over summer, you and your dog can take the water taxi that crosses Echo Lake, and shorten your hike by 5 miles. A wilderness permit is required for this hike. From South Lake Tahoe Y, drive south on Hwy 50 for 9.6 miles and turn right on Echo Lakes Road. Continue to an intersection and turn left. Park in the upper lot at the Echo Lakes Resort. The water taxi leaves from the boat dock at the Echo Lakes Resort. For information on the water taxi, call (530) 659-7207.

Ralston Peak Trail

8 Miles Roundtrip– Moderate

This scenic hike into Desolation Wilderness gives you beautiful views of Horsetail Falls, one of the most breathtaking waterfalls in Lake Tahoe. A wilderness permit is required for this hike. From South Lake Tahoe Y, drive 13.5 miles south on Hwy 50 and turn right at Camp Sacramento. Drive down this dirt road and park at the church. The Ralston Peak Trailhead is on the left side of the road.

Bonnie, Dalmation

Fountain Place Trail
4 Miles Roundtrip– Moderate
This trail passes through Fountain Place, an open meadow with beautiful wildflowers in spring. The climb is short and steep, with over 1700 feet of elevation gain. Enjoy the views from the top. From South Lake Tahoe Y, drive south on Hwy 50 for 4 miles and turn left on Pioneer Road. Turn right on Oneidas Street and drive to the end, where it becomes a Forest Service Road. Continue on this road until the pavement ends, approximately 4 miles. Park and follow the dirt road.

Freel Meadows Trail
12 Miles Roundtrip– Difficult
This scenic trail takes you along creeks, through dense forests and beside large granite slabs. You will end up at Hellhole Vista, where you can enjoy beautiful views of the Carson Range. From South Lake Tahoe Y, drive south on Hwy 50 for 4.5 miles to the stop light. Turn left on Hwy 89 and drive south for 5.5 miles to the Big Meadows Trailhead. Park in the main trailhead parking area. From the Big Meadow Trailhead, follow the blue diamonds that mark the Tahoe Rim Trail. Continue and follow the signs to Freel Meadows and Hellhole Vista.

Lake Margaret Trail
5 Miles Roundtrip– Easy
This trail takes you through forests of Pine and meadows of wildflowers. This is a great spot for a picnic and a swim. The trail is marked with white diamonds and arrows. From South Lake Tahoe Y, drive 4.5 miles south on Hwy 50 to the stop light. Turn left on Hwy 89 and drive south for 11 miles to Hwy 88. Drive towards Carson Pass for 13.6 miles and turn right at a paved road between Caples Lake and Kirkwood Ski Resort. Park near the Lake Margaret Trailhead.

Big Meadows Trail

6 Miles Roundtrip– Moderate

This trail takes you through a large, open meadow that's filled with beautiful wildflowers in spring. A creek follows the trail, which your dog will enjoy cooling off in on a hot summer day. The trail comes out at Round Lake, which is lined with large granite boulders. Bring a leash, you will need to cross the highway. From South Lake Tahoe Y, drive south on Hwy 50 for 4.5 miles to the stop light. Turn left on Hwy 89 and drive south for 5.5 miles to the Big Meadows Trailhead. Park and follow the trail at the south side of the lot. Safely cross the highway and find the trail on the other side of the road.

Emigrant Lake Trail

8 Miles Roundtrip– Moderate

The trail follows the shoreline of Caples Lake then climbs along Emigrant Creek. After passing through an open meadow and dense forest, you will arrive at Emigrant Lake which is surrounded by large granite boulders. Beautiful views of Kirkwood Ski Resort. From South Lake Tahoe Y, drive 4.5 miles south on Hwy 50 to the stop light. Turn left and follow Hwy 89 south for 11 miles to Hwy 88. Follow Hwy 88 towards Carson Pass 13.5 miles to the parking area, just past Caples Lake. Park and begin hiking at the Emigrant Lake Trailhead at the south end of the parking lot.

Animals are such agreeable friends,
they ask no questions,
they pass no criticisms.

–George Elliot

MOUNTAIN BIKING

Dusty, Weimaraner

Truckee

Carr, Feely and Lindsey Lakes Trails

There are miles and miles of hiking and mountain biking trails in this area, all that allow dogs. You will pass by many small lakes, including Lindsey Lake, Feely Lake, Milk Lake, Hidden Lake and Island Lake, where you can swim out to one of many islands. Be cautious of hikers. The following are some of the trails in this area:

Rock Lake– 8.5 Miles Roundtrip. Turn towards "Lindsey Lakes" on the road into the campground. Park at the campground and follow the fire road.

Penner Lake– 6.5 Miles Roundtrip. Turn towards "Carr and Feely Lake" on the road into the campground. Park in the lot and begin down the fire road on the south side of the campground. Follow the signs for Round Lake Trail to Crooked Lakes Trail. Continue on this trail to Penner Lake.

Shotgun Lake– 8 Miles Roundtrip. Turn towards "Carr and Feely Lake" on the road to the campground. Park in the lot and begin down the fire road at the south end of the campground. Follow Round Lake Trail and turn left on Grouse Ridge Trail, which will take you to Shotgun Lake.

DIRECTIONS: From Truckee, drive west on I-80 for 23 miles to the Nevada City Exit and go south. Drive for 4 miles on Route 20 and turn right on Bowman Road. Drive 8.5 miles to Forest Service Road #17. Turn right to follow the signs to Carr and Feely Lakes or left to go to "Lindsey Lakes". (Note: 4WD needed on this road).

Eagle Lakes/ Indian Springs Trails

There are many miles of hiking and mountain biking trails here that allow dogs. Be cautious of hikers. The following are 2 trails in this area:

Eagle Lakes– 6 Miles Roundtrip. This trail takes you to Eagle Lakes which is a great spot for camping.

Footfalls– 12 Miles Roundtrip. This trail leads to a beautiful waterfall and swimming hole. Use caution near the waterfall, the rocks can be slippery.

DIRECTIONS: From Truckee, drive west on I-80 for 20.5 miles to the Eagles Lake Exit. Go north for .5 miles and make a right on Eagle Lakes Road. Drive .2 miles on this dirt road to the parking area. Park here and continue up the dirt road to the Eagle Lakes Trailhead.

Mt. Lola

This strenuous 13 mile trail will take you through willow groves, open meadows, across creeks and ponds, and you will end up at 9,148 feet elevation with breathtaking panoramic vistas. From Truckee, head north on Hwy 89 for 14.5 miles to Henness Pass Road. Drive west for 1.5 miles to Jackson Meadow. Turn left at the sign for Independence Lake. After crossing the bridge, turn right on Old Henness Pass Road. Drive 3.3 miles to the Mt. Lola Trailhead. The trail is marked along the way with white arrows in the dirt and white diamonds on the trees.

North Shore

Western States Trail

There are about 10 miles of trails in this area for you and your dog to explore. Hop on that bike and enjoy the challenging uphill and the exhilarating downhill of this ride, which has beautiful views of the lake. From Tahoe City, drive north on Hwy 89 for 4.5 miles to the parking area by the Alpine Meadows Bridge on the left side of the road. Park and start down the paved bike path under the bridge, heading north and follow the signs to the Western States Trail.

Squaw Valley

Grab your bike and your dog and head for Squaw Valley. You can take the tram to the top and mountain bike with your dog on one of the numerous trails. From Tahoe City, drive 5 miles north on Hwy 89 and turn left on Squaw Valley Road. Park in the lot, and head towards the tram. Dogs must be leashed on the tram. $14 for adults, dogs are free. For more information, call (530) 583-6985.

Gracy, Black German Shepherd

Mount Watson Peak Trail

There are about 11 miles of trails and fire roads throughout this area. Check out the views at the top of Mount Watson! From Tahoe City, drive east on Hwy 28 for 2.5 miles and turn left on Fabian Way (just before the Shell Gas Station). Turn right on Village Road and left on Country Club Drive. Drive to the Lakeview Nordic Ski Area and park by the building. From the parking lot, go past the gate and down the fire road.

Martis Peak Trail

For an intermediate ride, bike 6 miles roundtrip to Martis Peak Lookout. For a more advanced ride, bike 12 miles roundtrip to the top of Mt. Baldy. Enjoy panoramic lakeviews of all of Lake Tahoe from this trail. From Tahoe City, drive east on Hwy 28 for 9 miles and turn left on Hwy 267. Drive just past Brockway Summit, and look for a dirt road on your right. Park at the entrance and follow the dirt road.

West Shore

Page Meadows

There are about 14 miles of trails in this area that will take you to scenic Page Meadows. Be cautious of hikers. From Tahoe City, drive south on Hwy 89 for .5 miles and turn right on Granlibakken Road. Turn left on Rawhide Drive and park at the end of the road. Go through the gates and along the fire road.

Ward Creek Canyon

This moderate 12 mile trail will take you to the top of Twin Peaks with views of Lake Tahoe, Ward Creek Canyon, and the Granite Chief Wilderness. From Tahoe City, drive south on Hwy 89 for 3.2 miles and turn right on Pineland Drive. Turn left on Twin Peaks Road, then follow the signs to Ward Creek Canyon. Drive to the Forest Service Road 15N62 and park. Start your ride left down the forest service road and follow the signs for Twin Peaks Trail.

Blackwood Canyon Road

There are about 15 miles of paved road for your biking pleasure. The road is level for the first 2.5 miles and then gets steep. Be cautious of cars, this area can get busy over summer. From Tahoe City, drive south on Hwy 89 for 4 miles to Blackwood Canyon Road (Kaspian Campground). There is a parking area on the right.

Barker Pass

There are almost 30 miles of trails in this area, off of Blackwood Canyon Road. Follow the trails to Ellis Lake and Ellis Peak. Be cautious of hikers. From Tahoe City, drive south on Hwy 89 for 4 miles to Blackwood Canyon Road (Kaspian Campground). Continue on Blackwood Canyon Road for 2.5 miles, until the road splits. Instead of following the paved road over the bridge, continue straight on the dirt road. There will be parking on the right. Begin down the fire road through the gate.

General Creek

This 6 mile trail is nice and level, perfect for the kids and the dog. From Tahoe City, drive 9.2 miles south on Hwy 89 to the General Creek Campground. There is a $3 fee at the entrance gate. Park in the visitor's parking lot. Begin down the paved bike path and veer right at the dirt trail. Maps available at the entrance gate.

Incline Village

Ophir Creek Trail

This is a great spot for children. The trail is 3 miles each way, and is almost completely level. This trail takes you through Tahoe Meadows, where you can enjoy the wildflowers, and your dog can enjoy the creek that follows along the trail. From Incline Village, drive north on Hwy 431 (Mount Rose Hwy) for 6.5 miles. You will see a large open meadow on your right. Park on the side of the road and find the trail by the creek.

Marlette Lake – Flume Trail

There are 16 miles of trails in this area for mountain biking with your dog. You'll start at Spooner Lake, and continue up past Marlette Lake to the Flume Trail. The trail comes out by the Ponderosa Ranch, so either leave one car there, or return to where you started. From Incline Village, drive south on Hwy 28 for approximately 12 miles to Spooner Lake- Nevada State Park. There is a $5 fee at the entrance gate. Park and follow the signs for Marlette Lake/ Flume Trail.

South Lake Tahoe

Angora Lakes Trail

This easy, 8 mile roundtrip bike ride follows a fire road to Angora Lakes. Be cautious of off-road vehicles. Boat rentals are available at the lake. From the South Lake Tahoe Y, drive north on Hwy 89 for 3 miles. Turn left on Fallen Leaf Lake Road and left on Tahoe Mountain Road. Park near Angora Ridge Road, which is a dirt road.

Lake Margaret Trail

This trail is easy and fun. Five miles roundtrip with many hills and dips along the way. Be cautious of hikers. The trail is marked with white diamonds and arrows. From South Lake Tahoe Y, drive south for 4.5 miles on Hwy 50 to the stop light. Turn left on Hwy 89 and drive south for 11 miles to Hwy 88. Drive towards Carson Pass for 13.6 miles and turn right at a paved road between Caples Lake and Kirkwood Ski Resort. Park near the Lake Margaret Trailhead.

Mr. Toad's Wild Ride

This 16 mile roundtrip ride is steep at times and can be difficult. Be cautious of slippery rocks. From the South Lake Tahoe Y, drive south on Hwy 50 for 4 miles and turn left on Pioneer Road. Turn right on Oneidas Street and drive through the gate, and continue until the road becomes a paved forest service road. Park near the Saxon Creek Bridge. Begin your ride up the paved road, follow the trail through the gate and continue on the dirt road.

*My idea of good poetry
is any dog doing anything.*

–J. Allen Boone

CROSS COUNTRY SKIING

Baxter, Black Lab / Dalmation Mix

Truckee

Donner Memorial State Park

Dogs are not allowed on the main groomed cross country trail, but they are allowed on smaller side trails. A sno-park permit is needed to park here. Parking and permit available at the museum. From Truckee, take the Donner Lake Exit off of I-80 and follow signs to the park.

Big Bend

There are unmarked trails running all over this area near the Yuba River. Be cautious of snowmobiles. From Truckee drive west on I-80 for 17 miles to the Big Bend Exit. Turn left on Hampshire Rocks Road and park in the parking lot. Begin at the trailhead.

Sagehen Trail

This unmarked trail is for more advanced cross country skiers and their dogs. Be cautious of snowmobiles. 5 Mile Loop. From Truckee, drive north on Hwy 89 for 8 miles to Sagehen Summit.
Park in the lot on the west side of the road.

Cabin Creek Trail

This trail has some steep areas and is for more advanced cross country skiers. Be cautious of snowmobiles. 9 Mile Loop. From Truckee, drive south on Hwy 89 for 3 miles to Cabin Creek Road. Turn right and drive 1 mile to the trailhead. Park on the side of the road.

North Shore

Martis Peak Trail

This intermediate trail is unmarked and continues for 3.5 miles (one way). Enjoy panoramic lakeviews of all of Lake Tahoe from this trail. From Tahoe City, drive east for 9 miles on Hwy 28 and turn left on Hwy 267. Drive north for 3.8 miles and turn left at the dirt turnout and park(.5 miles south of Brockway Summit). Cross Hwy 267 and start up the dirt road. Follow the signs for the Tahoe Rim Trail and veer left at the junction.

North Tahoe Regional Park

Enjoy beautiful lakeviews while cross country skiing with your dog on one of the many trails in this 300-acre park. Be cautious of snowmobiles. From Tahoe City, head east on Hwy 28, for 8.2 miles. Turn left on National Ave, and left on Donner Road. Follow the road to the park. $3 parking fee. For more information, call (530) 546-7248 or (530) 546-5043.

West Shore

Page Meadows

This unmarked trail for intermediates will take you and your dog to a big open meadow. From Tahoe City, drive south on Hwy 89 for about 3 miles. Turn right on Pine St. and veer right on Tahoe Park Heights Drive. Continue up the steep hill (you may need 4WD or chains) and turn right on Big Pine Drive. Make your first left on Silver Tip Drive. Go to the end of the paved road and park. The trail starts at the end of Silver Tip Drive.

Blackwood Canyon Road

This road is gated off over winter. The first 2.5 miles are flat, a great spot for beginners. If you would like more of a challenge, the trail continues another 7 miles and gets steeper and more difficult. Be cautious of snowmobiles. From Tahoe City, drive south on Hwy 89 for 3 miles to Blackwood Canyon Road, near the Kaspian Recreation Area. You will find the parking area on the right. A sno-park permit is needed to park here.

McKinney Rubicon Springs

This trail is unmarked and will take you through the forest and past several small lakes. Be cautious of snowmobiles. 6 Miles Roundtrip. From Tahoe City, drive south on Hwy 89 for approximately 9 miles and turn right on McKinney Rubicon Springs Road. Veer left to Bellvue Drive and turn right on McKinney Road. Turn left on McKinney Rubicon Springs Road. The trail begins at the end of the road.

Incline Village

Diamond Peak Cross Country Trails

Diamond Peak offers day passes or season passes for your dog. Enjoy 19 miles of well groomed trails, with 20% beginner trails, 50% intermediate trails, and 30% advanced trails. Dogs may join you cross country skiing all day Tuesday and Thursday, and 3:00pm to 4:30pm all other days. This day pass and season pass will also allow your dog access to the Diamond Peak snowplay area. $3 for a day pass and $25 for a season pass. For more information, call (702) 832-1177.

Tahoe Meadows

This large, flat meadow is a great spot for you and your dog to cross country ski. There are about 6 miles of trails. Be cautious of snowmobiles. From Incline Village, head west on Hwy 28 to Hwy 431 (Mount Rose Highway). Turn right and drive for 6.5 miles to the large flat meadow on the right side of the road and park.

South Lake Tahoe

Taylor Creek Sno-Park
There are trails for all level of cross country skier in this sno-park. No snowmobiles allowed on these trails. From the South Lake Tahoe Y, drive north on Hwy 89 for 3.5 miles to the sno-park. A sno-park permit is needed to park here.

Fountain Place
There are six miles of trails (one way) for the more advanced cross country skier. Be cautious of snowmobilers. From South Lake Tahoe Y, drive south on Hwy 50 for 4 miles and turn left on Pioneer Road. Turn right on Oneidas Street and drive to the end, where it becomes a Forest Service Road. Continue on this road until the pavement ends, approximately 4 miles. The trail starts at the end of the road.

Angora Road
This trail is 8 miles roundtrip and is for the intermediate cross country skier. You will ski through woods and past several small lakes. Be cautious of snowmobilers. From South Lake Tahoe Y, drive south for 2.5 miles on Hwy 50 and turn right on Tahoe Mountain Road. Turn right on Glenmore Way and left on Dundee Circle. Turn left and follow to the end of the road, where the trail begins down a fire road on your left.

Echo Lakes
This trail is for intermediate cross country skiers and their dogs. There are many trails in this area, most which lead to Upper and Lower Echo Lakes. A map of the trails can be picked up at the Forest Service Office. A sno-park permit is needed to park here. From South Lake Tahoe Y, drive south on Hwy 50 for 9.6 miles and turn right on Echo Lakes Road. Park in the Echo Lakes Sno-Park area.

Grass Lake Meadow
This is a great spot for beginners. There are about 3 miles of flat, open meadow for you and your dogs. From South Lake Tahoe Y, drive south for 4.5 miles on Hwy 50 to the stop light. Turn left on Hwy 89 and drive to Luther Pass and park on the side of the road.

The dog is a true philosopher.

—Socrates

SLEDDING HILLS

Szabo, St. Bernard Mix

Truckee

Truckee
This is an unofficial snow sledding spot that is used by locals. From downtown Truckee drive 1/4 mile west on Donner Pass Road.

Glenshire
This is an unofficial snow play area. From downtown Truckee, drive east on Donner Pass Road and turn right on Glenshire Drive. The sledding hill is down 5 miles on the west side of the road.

North Shore

Tahoe City
This is an unofficial snow sledding spot that is used by locals. From Tahoe City Y, drive south on Hwy 89 for 1/8 mile. The sledding hill is on the lake side of the highway.

Brockway Summit
This is an unofficial snow sledding spot that is used by locals. From Tahoe City, drive east on Hwy 28 for 9 miles and turn left on Hwy 267. The sledding hill is located .8 miles south of Northstar on Hwy 267.

North Tahoe Regional Park
There are both beginner and intermediate sledding hills at this snow park. From Tahoe City, head east on Hwy 28 for 8.2 miles. Turn left on National Ave, and left on Donner Road. Follow the road to the park. Parking- $3. Sledding- $5 per person with sled rental, $3 per person without sled rental. For more information, call (530) 546-7248 or (530) 546-6115.

Incline Village

Tahoe Meadows
This is an unofficial snow sledding spot that is often used by locals. From Incline Village, head west on Hwy 28 to Hwy 431 (Mount Rose Highway). Turn right and drive for 6.5 miles to the parking area on the right side of the road.

Diamond Peak Snow Play Area

Diamond Peak offers day passes or season passes for your dog. This pass will allow your dog at the Diamond Peak snowplay area, and on the Diamond Peak cross country skiing trails. Dogs may join you in the snowplay area or cross country skiing all day Tuesday and Thursday, and 3:00pm to 4:30pm all other days. $3 for a day pass and $25 for a season pass. For more information, call (702) 832-1177.

Spooner Summit

This unofficial snow sledding spot is steep, so don't bring your small children. From Incline Village drive south on Hwy 28 for about 9 miles to the junction with Hwy 50. The sledding hill is on the west side of the highway.

Incline Village

This unofficial snow sledding spot is great for beginners, and is located on the Incline Village Golf Course. The hill is on the driving range, next to The Chateau. From Incline Village, drive east on Hwy 28 and turn left on Country Club Drive.

South Lake Tahoe

Echo Summit Sno-Park

This sno-park has a large area for snow sledding. From South Lake Tahoe Y, drive south on Hwy 50 about 10 miles to Meyers. Look for the Echo Summit Sno-Park sign and park in the lot. A sno-park permit is needed to park here.

Taylor Creek Sno-Park

This sno-park has a small sledding hill. From South Lake Tahoe Y, drive north on Hwy 89 for 3 miles. The sno-park will be on your left near Camp Richardson. A sno-park permit needed to park here.

*Lord, help me to become
the kind of person my dog thinks I am.*

—Unknown

SWIMMING AREAS

Buddy, Golden Retriever

Truckee

Martis Creek Lake

This lake is a great spot to picnic while your dog takes a swim. From Truckee, drive south on Hwy 267 for approximately 5 miles. Turn left at the Martis Creek Lake sign, and drive .5 miles to the lake.

Truckee River in Glenshire

A nice place for a quick dip to cool your dog on a hot summer day. From Truckee, drive east on Donner Pass Road past downtown and turn right on Glenshire Drive. Go 4.5 miles and turn right just past Glenshire Bridge. Follow the dirt road and park near the river.

North Shore

Coon St. Beach

This beach is small, but large enough to make any water dog happy. Bring your lunch and eat at one of the picnic tables. From Tahoe City, drive east on Hwy 28 for 9.2 miles to Kings Beach, and turn left on Coon St.

Lake Forest Beach & Campground

This rocky dog beach is not pretty, but hey, it's water. There is a boat ramp next to the beach. From Tahoe City, drive east on Hwy 28 for approximately 2 miles and turn right on Lake Forest Road. Turn at the Coast Guard sign and veer right to the campground area. The beach is on your left.

Tahoe State Recreation Area

This campground in Tahoe City has its own private beach which allows dogs. Located just east of the Safeway Shopping Center in Tahoe City.

Watson Lake

A great place for you to have a picnic, and your dog to have a swim. You'll need 4-wheel drive to get to this lake. From Tahoe City, drive east on Hwy 28 for 9 miles and turn left on Hwy 267. Drive to the top of Brockway Summit and turn left at the summit on the dirt road. Follow the dirt road for 6.5 miles and turn left at another dirt road, marked 16N50 or 6/30. This will take you to Watson Lake.

William B Layton Memorial Park

This 3 acre park in Tahoe City allows dogs to roll on its grassy lawns, and swim at its rocky beach. Enjoy some lunch at one of the picnic tables. Located right in Tahoe City behind the Bridgetender Bar & Grill.

West Shore

Blackwood Canyon

The landscape here is breathtaking! You and your dog can hike upstream, or stay and play in the water hole. From Tahoe City, drive south on Hwy 89 for 4.2 miles and turn right on Blackwood Canyon Road. Veer to the left and park near the bridge.

Hurricane Beach

This 'designated dog beach' is about 50 feet of beach right on the highway. If your dog tends to wander stay away from this beach. From Tahoe City, drive south on Hwy 89 for approximately 4 miles.

Incline Village

Incline Village Beach

The beautiful Incline Village Beach is open to dogs in the off season, November through May. There are doggie dispensers with free scoopers to encourage you to clean up after your dog. From downtown Incline Village, drive east on Hwy 28 and turn right on Country Club Drive. Turn right on Lakeshore Blvd and turn left into the second gated beach.

Akala, Malamute Mix

East Shore Beaches

The East Shore has some of the most spectacular beaches on the lake. You and your dog can swim out to one of the many rocks that stick out from the crystal clear water. From Incline Village, drive east on Hwy 28, past the residential area. The beaches are scattered along the highway and are hard to see. When you see cars parked on the side of the road, park and walk towards the lake. There will be a trail that leads to the beach.

South Lake Tahoe

Kiva Beach

This large, sandy beach has restrooms and picnic tables. Dogs must be leashed. From South Lake Tahoe Y, drive north on Hwy 89 for 2.5 miles to Kiva Beach.

Tallac Historic Site

Leashed dogs are allowed on the grounds and at the beach of the Tallac Historic Site. While you are there, check out the three historic estates: Pope, Valhalla, and Baldwin. From South Lake Tahoe Y, drive north on Hwy 89 for approximately 3 miles and turn right at the sign for the Tallac Historic Site.

Echo Lakes

This is a great spot for you and your dog to picnic and swim. There is a water taxi that can take both of you across the lake. From South Lake Tahoe Y, drive south on Hwy 50 for 9.6 miles and turn right on Echo Lakes Road. Continue to an intersection and turn left. Park in the upper lot at the Echo Lakes Resort. The water taxi leaves from the boat dock at the Echo Lakes Resort. The water taxi usually runs between Memorial Day and Labor Day, from 8 am to 5 pm. $6 per person, $3 per dog. For more information, call (530) 659-7207.

Fallen Leaf Lake

This scenic lake is a great spot for picnicking, swimming, fishing, camping and biking. From the South Lake Tahoe Y, drive north on Hwy 89 and turn left on Fallen Leaf Lake Road. Follow the road past the campground to the Fallen Leaf Lake Trailhead.

*Not Carnegie, Vanderbilt and Astor together
could have raised enough money
to buy a quarter share in my little dog.*

–Ernest Thompson Seton

FISHING SPOTS

Ritter, Timberwolf / Lab Mix

Truckee

Truckee River in Glenshire

The fishing is great in the Truckee River. Catch and release only in this area. From Truckee, drive east on Donner Pass Road, past downtown and turn right on Glenshire Drive. Go 4.5 miles and turn right just past Glenshire Bridge. Follow the dirt road and park near the river.

Martis Creek Lake

This lake is a popular spot for fly fishing and only allows catch and release. It's known for its Lahonton cutthroat trout, German brown trout, and Eagle Lake-strain rainbow trout. Artificial lures and flies with barbless hooks only. From Truckee, drive south on Hwy 267 for 6 miles. Turn left at the Martis Creek Lake sign, and drive .5 miles to the lake.

Sparky, Yellow Lab

Boca Reservoir

This large reservoir is stocked with kokanee salmon, rainbow trout and brown trout. From Truckee, drive 7 miles east on I-80 and take the Hirschdale Exit. Drive north on Stampede Dam Road to the lake.

Stampede Reservoir

This popular fishing spot is filled with kokanee salmon, mountain whitefish, rainbow trout, Mackinaw trout, brook trout and brown trout. From Truckee, drive 7 miles east on I-80 to the Hirschdale Exit. Drive north on Stampede Dam Road for 8 miles to the Stampede Reservoir.

Prosser Creek Reservoir

Rainbow and brown trout inhabit this lake. Trolling is good along the shore. From Truckee, drive north on Hwy 89 for 2.5 miles and turn right on Prosser Dam Road.

Sagehen Creek

You'll be likely to catch rainbow, brook or brown trout in this creek. Catch and release only in this area. From Truckee, drive north on Hwy 89 for 7.5 miles to where the creek crosses under the highway.

West Shore

Desolation Wilderness Lakes

There are numerous lakes in the Desolation Wilderness area that have great fishing. You will need to hike in to get to the lakes. Check out the Hiking Trails section of this book for trail directions to get to these great fishing spots: Velma Lakes, Granite Lake, Crag Lake, and Susie Lake.

Nookers, Great Pyrenees

Incline Village

Spooner Lake

This small lake is filled with cutthroat trout. Catch and release only. From Incline Village, drive south on Hwy 28 approximately 9 miles to Spooner Lake at the Nevada State Park.

South Lake Tahoe

Fallen Leaf Lake

There is an abundant supply kokanee salmon and Mackinaw trout in this large lake. From the South Lake Tahoe Y, drive north on Hwy 89 and turn left on Fallen Leaf Lake Road.

Taylor Creek

Fallen Leaf Lake releases water periodically into Taylor Creek. Along with kokanee salmon, the creek is filled with rainbow and brown trout. From South Lake Tahoe Y, drive north on Hwy 89 for 3.2 miles to the Taylor Creek Visitors Center. Park and walk towards the creek.

Echo Lakes

Upper and Lower Echo Lakes are connected by a small channel. Both are filled with kokanee salmon, cutthroat trout, rainbow trout and brook trout. From South Lake Tahoe Y, drive south on Hwy 50 for 9.6 miles and turn right on Echo Lakes Road. Continue to an intersection and turn left. Park in the upper lot at the Echo Lakes Resort.

Dogs have given us their absolute all.
We are the center of their universe.
We are the focus of their love and faith and trust.
They serve us in return for scraps.
It is without a doubt the best deal man has ever made.

–Roger Caras

OTHER DOGGIE ADVENTURES

Zoey, Black Lab

Truckee

Dairy Queen Puppy Cup

Drive through the Dairy Queen in Truckee, and receive a free 'puppy cup' of vanilla ice cream for your dog. 11355 Donner Pass Road, Donner Plaza, Truckee (530) 587-7055.

North Shore

Squaw Valley Tram Ride

During the summer months, you and your dog can take the tram to the top of Squaw Valley. At the top, you will find fields of wildflowers and many trails to explore. Dogs must be leashed on the tram. The tram costs $14 for adults, and after 5pm, it's $5. Dogs are free. For more information, call (530) 583-6985.

Rafting Down the Truckee

What could be better than a relaxing summer day, rafting down the Truckee River with your dog. Raft rentals are available at Mountain Air Sports, located at 205 River Road, along Hwy 89 and Fanny Bridge Raft Rentals, located near Fanny Bridge. Only some dogs are allowed, depending on their size and the sharpness of their claws. You may want to call first. Mountain Air Sports (530) 583-5606, Fanny Bridge Raft Rentals (530) 583-0123.

Fishing Charters and Lake Tours

The six hour fishing charters go out in the morning and afternoon, and run $65 per person. Tackle is supplied. Lake tours are $70 per hour and include a BBQ lunch on the boat. Two dogs allowed on the boat. For more information, contact Pete at The Reel Deal Sportfishing & Lake Tours (530) 581-0924, or (530) 206-REEL.

Double Dawg Jawg

This annual fund raiser is held by the Naughty Dawg Saloon and Grill in Tahoe City. It benefits the needy animals at the Pet Network of Lake Tahoe. The 2 mile jog starts at the Naughty Dawg and loops behind the Tahoe City Golf Course. This loop can be done twice if desired. A $15 fee gets you and your dog into the race, and gets you a t-shirt. After, there is a raffle with great prizes from local sponsors. For more information, call the Naughty Dawg at (530) 583-DAWG.

Naughty Dawg Monster Dog Pull

The Naughty Dawg Saloon & Grill puts on this contest annually in Tahoe City as part of Snowfest, usually the end of February. The dogs are harnessed to one of several different sizes of beer kegs, depending on weight. The first dog to pull the keg of beer over the finish line wins. All dogs that enter receive prizes. $5 to enter your dog. The contest benefits the Pet Network of Lake Tahoe. For more information, call The Naughty Dawg at (530) 581-DAWG or Snowfest at (530) 583-7625.

Dress Up Your Dog Contest

This contest is put on by the Agate Bay Animal Hospital annually in North Lake Tahoe during Snowfest, usually the end of February. The categories include: Cutest, Looks Most Like Owner, Best Group Act, Most Original, and Looks Most Like Famous Person. Prizes are given to all who enter. $5 to enter your dog. For more information, call the Agate Bay Animal Hospital at (530) 546-7522 or Snowfest at (530) 583-7625.

Sierra Mountain Doggie Camp

When you go away on a trip, instead of sending your dog to a kennel, send him to doggie camp. Your dog will hike in the Sierra and swim in Lake Tahoe. He'll come home with a photo album of all his doggie adventures. Airfare can be arranged. For more information, call Suzy Scully at (530) 581-0623, or e-mail her at www.sierradoggiecamp.com

Wedding Bells

You can't get married without your best friend! A Chapel by the River, can accommodate your desire to have your furry friend present on your wedding day. 115 West Lake Blvd, Tahoe City (530) 581-2757.

Mariah, Chocolate Lab Pup

West Shore

Emerald Bay Boat-In Camp
One of the most popular campsites around, this spot is complete with a large pier and a long sandy beach. Check out Vikingsholm during the day, and camp here at night. Dogs must be leashed and are not allowed in Vikingsholm. Closed for the winter. 20 sites, $10 fee. Located on the north side of Emerald Bay. For more information, call (530) 525-7277.

Incline Village

Annual Pet Walk
This fund raiser is held by the Pet Network of Lake Tahoe every September in Incline Village. It benefits needy pets and helps find them new homes. There are food booths, crafts, dog contests and demonstrations. A $15 entrance fee gets you a Pet Network t-shirt, and gets your dog a bandanna and a bag of treats. For more information, call the Pet Network at (702) 832-4404.

Doggie Season Pass at Diamond Peak
Get a day pass or season pass for your dog at Diamond Peak for the cross country and snow play areas. $3 for a day pass, $25 for a season pass. Dogs are allowed in these areas all day Tuesday and Thursdays, and every other day between 3:00 and 4:30 pm. For more information, call Diamond Peak at (702) 832-1177.

South Lake Tahoe

Echo Lakes Boat Tour

Over summer you and your dog can get a guided tour of Echo Lakes. This 1.5 hour tour is complete with a Forest Service Naturalist, ready to tell you and your dog all that you ever wanted to know about this spectacular area. The tours are Tuesday and Thursday mornings at 10:00 am. The boat acts as a water taxi the rest of the day, bringing hikers back and forth across the 2.5 mile lake. The water taxi hours are 8 am to 5 pm. The boat usually runs between Memorial Day and Labor Day, depending on the weather. From South Lake Tahoe Y, drive south on Hwy 50 for 9.6 miles and turn right on Echo Lakes Road. Continue to an intersection and turn left. Park in the upper lot at the Echo Lakes Resort. The boat tour and water taxi leaves from the boat dock at the Echo Lakes Resort. For more information, call Echo Lakes at (530) 659-7207.

Taylor Creek Visitors Center

Come see Mother Nature at her finest. There are guided nature trails, daily discussion groups about different aspects of Lake Tahoe, even a campfire program with discussions, songs and marshmallows. And your dog is welcome at all of them! There is a lot to explore here, including an underground stream profile chamber. Dogs must be leashed. From South Lake Tahoe Y, drive north on Hwy 89 for 3.5 miles at turn right into the Visitors Center. For more information about activities and program schedules, call (530) 573-2600 or (530) 573-2694.

Kokanee Salmon Festival

This 2 day festival is held annually in October at the Taylor Creek Visitors Center to celebrate the spawning of the Kokanee Salmon. There are special events, great food and music, fun contests, and interpretive programs. Grab the kids and the dog and make a day of it! For more information, call (530) 573-2600.

Sportfishing Charters

Your dog will love feeling the wind through his hair as you set out for a day of fishing in Lake Tahoe. These 1/2 day or full day trips run year round, with all of the fishing gear furnished. Captain Dean and Captain John can accommodate any size party, with their 7 fishing boats. Located in the Ski Run Marina. For more information, call (530) 541-5448 or (800) 696-7797.

Kirkwood BBQ and Campfire

Every Saturday evening throughout the summer months, Kirkwood Ski & Summer Resort has a barbecue dinner followed by a campfire with games, songs and story telling. It's a great time for you, your kids, and your dog. For more information on the campfire activities or lodging, call (800) 967-7500.

Wedding Bells

You can't walk down the aisle without your best friend at your side! The Chapel of the Bells is happy to have your furry friend join you on this joyous day. 2700 Lake Tahoe Blvd, South Lake Tahoe (800) 247-4333, or (530) 544-1112.

Thirsty Duck Bar & Grill

Friday night, bring your dog to the outside BBQ (ribs and chicken) during the summer months. Full bar outside. 400 Dorla Ct, Zephyr Cove (702) 588-3899.

Happiness is a warm puppy.

–Charles Schulz

DOG SERVICES

Benson, Mastiff Pup

PET SHOPS

Truckee

Mickey's Pet Shop
Westgate Shopping Center, Truckee (530) 587-1675

Gateway Pets
1120 Donner Pass Road, Truckee (530) 582-0608

North Shore

C&C Pet Stop
950 North Lake Blvd, Tahoe City (530) 581-4828

Incline Village

Lakeview Pets
873 Tahoe Blvd, Incline Village (702) 833-3939

The Pet Shack
797 Southwood Blvd, Incline Village (702) 832-0500

South Lake Tahoe

Animal Works
2291 Lake Tahoe Blvd, SLK Tahoe (530) 541-3831

The Dog House & Cattery
260 Kingsbury Grade, Kingsbury (702) 588-4621

Pet Supermarket
1074 Emerald Bay Road, SLK Tahoe (530) 544-9133

Pet World
3336 Sandy Way, SLK Tahoe (530) 541-7387

The Pet Pantry
128 Market, Kingsbury (702) 588-2027

VETERINARIANS

Truckee

Donner-Truckee Veterinary Hospital
9701 North Shore Blvd, Truckee (530) 587-4366

Sierra Pet Clinic of Truckee
10411 River Park Place, Truckee (530) 587-7200

North Shore

North Lake Veterinary Clinic
2933 Lake Forest Rd, Tahoe City (530) 583-8587

Agate Bay Animal Hospital
8428 Trout Ave, Kings Beach (530) 546-7522

Incline Village

Incline Veterinary Hospital
880 Tanager, Incline Village (702) 831-0433

South Lake Tahoe

Alpine Animal Hospital
921 Emerald Bay Rd, SLK Tahoe (530) 541-4040

Alpine-Round Hill Animal Clinic
392 Dorla Ct, Elk Point (702) 588-8744

Emerald Bay Veterinary Hospital
1022 Emerald Bay Road, SLK Tahoe (530) 544-2518

Kingsbury Veterinary Hospital
183 Shady Ln, Stateline (702) 588-3828

Sierra Veterinary Hospital
3095 Hwy 50, SLK Tahoe (530) 542-1952

South Tahoe Veterinary Hospital
Homeopathic Veterinary Practice
964 Rubicon Tr, SLK Tahoe (530) 541-3551

DOG GROOMERS

Truckee

Gateway Pets
11200 Donner Pass Road, Truckee (530) 582-0608

Mickey's Pet Shop
11429 Donner Pass Road, Truckee (530) 587-1675

Sierra Pet Clinic of Truckee
10411 River Park Place, Truckee (530) 587-7200

North Shore

North Lake Veterinary Clinic
2993 Lake Forest Road, Tahoe City (530) 583-8587

Jo-Mar's Pet Coiffures
8775 North Lake Blvd, Kings Beach (530) 546-5756

Incline Village

The Pet Shack
797 Southwood Blvd, Incline Village (702) 832-0500

South Lake Tahoe

The Dog House and Cattery
260 Kingsbury Grade, Kingsbury (702) 588-4621

Four Paws Grooming & Boarding
979 Tallac Ave, SLK Tahoe (530) 542-2377

Jacki Wright's Mobile Dog & Cat Grooming
Mobile Dog and Cat Salon (530) 542-1777

Paw Spa
2494 Lake Tahoe Blvd, A-7 Pine Cone Plaza
(530) 544-PAWS

Pet World
3336 Sandy way, SLK Tahoe (530) 541-7387

Posh Paws
Mobile Dog Salon (702) 588-PAWS

Dog Kennels

Truckee

Bed & Breakfast For Pets
Highway 267, Truckee (530) 587-3596

Truckee-Sierra Boarding Kennel
Hwy 89 & Alder Creek Road, Truckee (530) 587-2678

North Shore

North Lake Veterinary Clinic
2933 Lake Forest Road, Tahoe City (530) 583-8587

Incline Village

Incline Veterinary Hospital
880 Tanager, Incline Village (702) 831-0433

South Lake Tahoe

Alpine Animal Hospital
921 Emerald Bay Rd, SLK Tahoe (530) 541-4040

Four Paws Grooming and Boarding
979 Tallac Ave, SLK Tahoe (530) 542-2377

Sierra Veterinary Hospital
3095 Hwy 50, SLK Tahoe (530) 542-1952

South Tahoe Veterinary Hospital
964 Rubicon Tr, SLK Tahoe (530) 541-3551

DOG SITTERS

Truckee

Pampered Pet Care
Marjie Aubrey (530) 587-2701

Pet Sitting Plus
(530) 582-4120

North Shore

Doggie Day Care & Overnight Boarding
Sue Kirk (530) 583-9537

Reining Cats and Dogs
Marjorie Ann Woodbridge (530) 525-9101

Jen's In-Home Pet Care
Jennifer Klair (530) 546-1323 or (702) 831-3754

High Sierra Pet Connection
Todd (530) 583-5324

Pet & Company
Leslie LaMantia (530) 546-4112

Incline Village

Jen's In-Home Pet Care
Jennifer Klair (530) 546-1323 or (702) 831-3754

Pet & Company
Leslie LaMantia (530) 546-4112

Incline Royal Pet Care
Pamela Schooley (702) 831-4694
Pet sitting, training, exercise, transportation, grooming, hotel sitting, from King's Beach to Incline Village.

South Lake Tahoe

Paws N Poseys
Linda Lafond, South Lake Tahoe, (702) 588-3712

Peace of Mind Home Services
Kelly, South Lake Tahoe, (530) 544-7877

The Pet Nanny
South Lake Tahoe, (530) 541-6475

DOG TRAINERS

Sun Dog Obedience
Margie Lapanja (530) 546-DOGS or (702) 832-4031
Truckee, North Shore, Incline Village

Beyond Obedience
Jeanie Collins (530) 587-4499
Canine Behavioral Consultant
Truckee

Guy Yeaman- Professional Dog Trainer
(702) 265-4530
North Shore, South Shore

The Dog Trainer
Sandra Hann (530) 546-0966
North Shore

Todd Webb
(530) 544-6302
South Shore

Petalk
Patricia Simonet (702) 831-8970
Animal Behaviorist
Truckee, North Shore, West Shore,
Incline Village, and South Shore

DOG FENCING

Tahoe Hidden Fencing
Brian & Patty Hansen (530) 582-5558

Invisible Fencing of Sierra
Truckee, (800) 727-1411

Alpine Fence Company
848 Tanager Bldg. G, Incline Village (702) 831-6231
Dog Runs, Dog Kennels

Tahoe Fence Company
South Lake Tahoe, (800) 332-2822
Dog Runs, Dog Kennels

South Shore Fence
1640 Apache Dr, South Lake Tahoe (530) 573-8923
Dog Runs, Dog Kennels

Lake Tahoe Dog Laws

In and around Lake Tahoe, Leash Laws require you to have your dog on leash and under voice control. A dog is 'at large' when he is under no supervision, without a leash or restraint and on someone else's property. Dogs will be picked up by an animal control officer when they are 'at large' and taken to a nearby animal shelter.

Truckee has a Control Law, which allows the dog to be off leash, but under visual and voice control. A dog will be picked up in this area for being 'at large' when he is unsupervised and on another's property.

Sno-Park Permits

Sno-Park permits are required for parking at designated Sno-Park areas. A day permit is $5 and a season permit is $25. Permits are available at the following locations:

Truckee:
Emigrant Trail Museum, Donner Memorial State Park (530) 587-3841

North Shore:
Alpenglow Sports, 415 North Lake Blvd, Tahoe City (530) 583-6917
AAA (Members) 7717 North Lake Blvd, Kings Beach (530) 546-4245

West Shore:
Homewood Hardware, 5405 West Lake Blvd, Homewood
(530) 525-6367

South Shore:
AAA (Members) 961 Emerald Bay Road, SLK Tahoe (530) 541-4434
South Tahoe Shell, 1020 Emerald Bay Rd, SLK Tahoe (530) 541-2720
Meyers Shell and Food Mart, 2950 Hwy 50, Meyers (530) 577-4533

Wilderness Permits

Wilderness permits are required when hiking or camping in Desolation Wilderness. There are two different permits, one for day users and one for overnight camping.

Day Use Permits
The day use permit is free and is available with self-registration, at most of the trailheads into Desolation Wilderness. They are also available at the Lake Tahoe Basin Management Office at 870 Emerald Bay Road, Suite #1, SLK Tahoe (530) 573-2600.

Overnight Use Permits
Those who plan to spend the night in Desolation Wilderness must register at the Lake Tahoe Basin Management Office in South Lake Tahoe. There is a quota system in effect to limit the number of overnight users in Desolation Wilderness. One permit is good for up to 15 people, and 700 permits is the limit per day. Half of the permits available can be reserved up to 90 days in advance, and the rest are issued that day on a first come, first serve basis. Open campfires are not allowed in Desolation Wilderness, use only portable gas stoves. For more information, contact the Lake Tahoe Basin Management Office at (530) 573-2600, 870 Emerald bay Rd, Suite #1, SLK Tahoe.

TAHOE DOG TIPS

WINTER TIPS

If your dog gets dry, itchy skin from the cold winter air, add a teaspoon of canola oil daily to their food. You will start seeing an improvement in your dog's coat in a few weeks.

Make sure to comb your dog's thick coat over winter. Dirt can get trapped against the skin and cause your dog to have skin irritations or skin diseases.

To remove mats from your dog's fir, sprinkle cornstarch on the mat, and the tangle should come right out.

During the winter, be aware that salting your icy driveway can burn the pads on your dog's feet.

Keep your dog from getting frost-bitten feet by keeping the hair in between his toes trimmed. This will prevent snow from accumulating between his toes and causing frostbite.

Some people will put anti freeze in their toilets over winter to keep the pipes from freezing. Be aware of this when bringing your dog into someone else's home.

During winter, dogs use up more energy keeping warm. Remember this during feeding time, a little extra food will help.

TAHOE DOG TIPS

SUMMER TIPS

Don't give your long haired dog a haircut over summer. That thick coat can actually keep him cooler.

To remove sap from your dog's fur, try either mayonnaise or Avon Skin-so-soft lotion.

Take your dog out for his walk in the morning or evening to avoid the heat.

Get a small wading pool and fill it with water. Your dog will enjoy cooling off on hot summer days.

Dogs will double their water intake during the hot summer months. Leave out an extra bowl of water out for them during this time.

Never leave your dog alone in a car during the summer. It only takes a few minutes for the temperature in your car to increase dramatically, which can be life-threatening to your dog.

Dogs can get sunburns and skin cancer. If your dog's in the sun most of the day, consider putting an SPF sunscreen on his nose and ears. Avoid sunscreens that contain zinc, they can be harmful to your dog if swallowed.

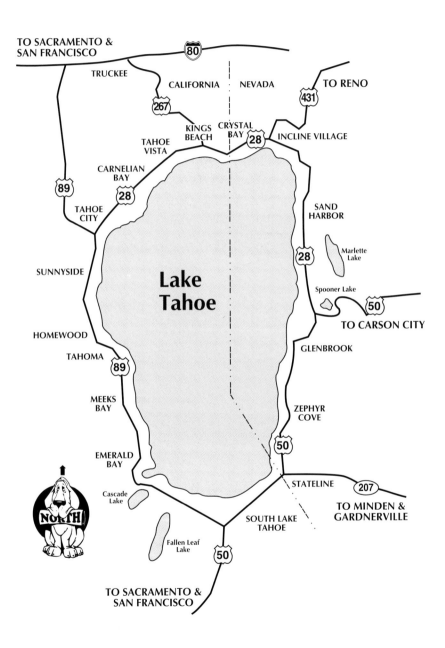

TO SACRAMENTO &
SAN FRANCISCO

80

TRUCKEE

CALIFORNIA · NEVADA

TO RENO

431

267

KINGS
BEACH

CRYSTAL
BAY

28

INCLINE VILLAGE

TAHOE
VISTA

CARNELIAN
BAY

28

89

TAHOE
CITY

SAND
HARBOR

Marlette
Lake

28

SUNNYSIDE

Lake
Tahoe

Spooner Lake

50

TO CARSON CITY

HOMEWOOD

GLENBROOK

TAHOMA

89

MEEKS
BAY

ZEPHYR
COVE

EMERALD
BAY

50

STATELINE

207

Cascade
Lake

TO MINDEN &
GARDNERVILLE

NORTH

SOUTH LAKE
TAHOE

Fallen Leaf
Lake

50

TO SACRAMENTO &
SAN FRANCISCO

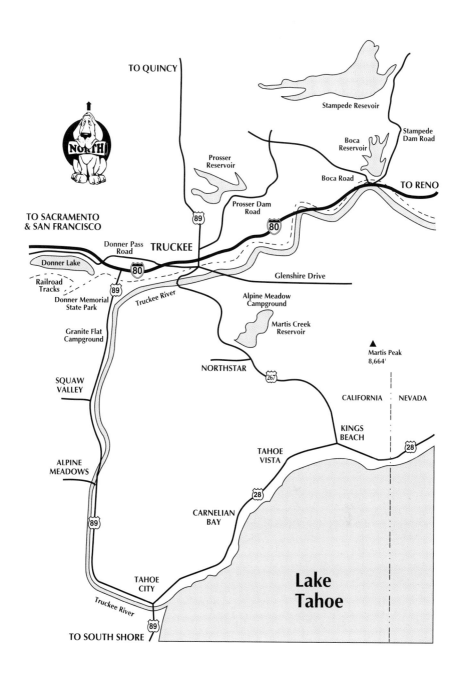

TO QUINCY

Stampede Resevoir

Stampede Dam Road

Boca Reservoir

Prosser Reservoir

Boca Road

TO RENO

Prosser Dam Road

89

80

TO SACRAMENTO & SAN FRANCISCO

Donner Pass Road

TRUCKEE

80

Donner Lake

Glenshire Drive

Railroad Tracks

89

Truckee River

Alpine Meadow Campground

Donner Memorial State Park

Martis Creek Reservoir

Granite Flat Campground

▲ Martis Peak 8,664'

NORTHSTAR

267

SQUAW VALLEY

CALIFORNIA · NEVADA

KINGS BEACH

28

ALPINE MEADOWS

TAHOE VISTA

89

28

CARNELIAN BAY

Lake Tahoe

TAHOE CITY

Truckee River

89

TO SOUTH SHORE

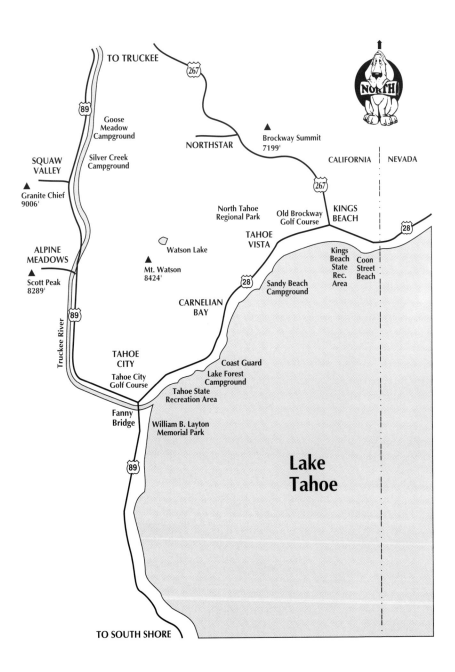

TO TRUCKEE

267

NORTH

89

Goose
Meadow
Campground

Silver Creek
Campground

NORTHSTAR

▲ Brockway Summit
7199'

CALIFORNIA | NEVADA

SQUAW
VALLEY

267

▲ Granite Chief
9006'

North Tahoe
Regional Park

Old Brockway
Golf Course

KINGS
BEACH

28

ALPINE
MEADOWS

◇ Watson Lake

TAHOE
VISTA

Kings
Beach
State
Rec.
Area

Coon
Street
Beach

▲ Mt. Watson
8424'

28

Sandy Beach
Campground

▲ Scott Peak
8289'

89

CARNELIAN
BAY

Truckee River

TAHOE
CITY

Coast Guard
Lake Forest
Campground

Tahoe City
Golf Course

Tahoe State
Recreation Area

Fanny
Bridge

William B. Layton
Memorial Park

89

**Lake
Tahoe**

TO SOUTH SHORE

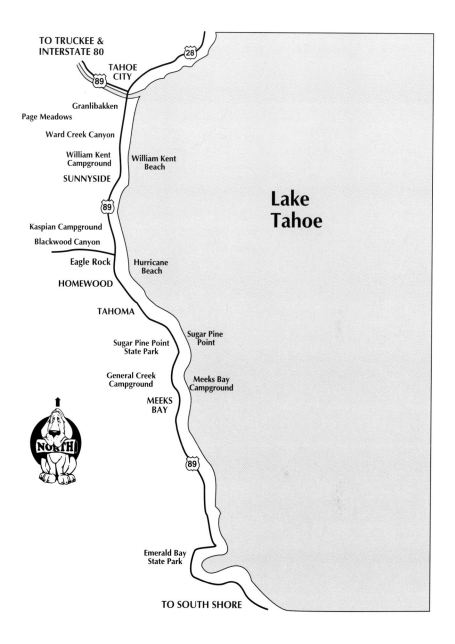

TO TRUCKEE &
INTERSTATE 80

28

TAHOE
CITY

89

Granlibakken

Page Meadows

Ward Creek Canyon

William Kent
Campground

William Kent
Beach

SUNNYSIDE

89

Lake
Tahoe

Kaspian Campground

Blackwood Canyon

Eagle Rock

Hurricane
Beach

HOMEWOOD

TAHOMA

Sugar Pine
Point

Sugar Pine Point
State Park

General Creek
Campground

Meeks Bay
Campground

MEEKS
BAY

NORTH

89

Emerald Bay
State Park

TO SOUTH SHORE

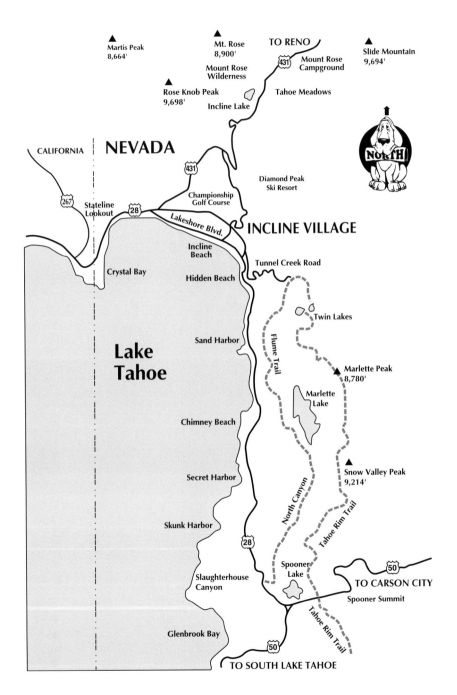

Martis Peak
8,664'

Mt. Rose
8,900'

Mount Rose
Wilderness

TO RENO

431

Mount Rose
Campground

Slide Mountain
9,694'

Rose Knob Peak
9,698'

Incline Lake

Tahoe Meadows

CALIFORNIA | NEVADA

Diamond Peak
Ski Resort

NORTH

431

267

28

Stateline
Lookout

Championship
Golf Course

Lakeshore Blvd.

INCLINE VILLAGE

Incline
Beach

Crystal Bay

Hidden Beach

Tunnel Creek Road

Twin Lakes

Sand Harbor

Flume Trail

Marlette Peak
8,780'

Lake
Tahoe

Marlette
Lake

Chimney Beach

Secret Harbor

Snow Valley Peak
9,214'

North Canyon

Tahoe Rim Trail

Skunk Harbor

28

Spooner
Lake

50

TO CARSON CITY

Slaughterhouse
Canyon

Spooner Summit

Tahoe Rim Trail

Glenbrook Bay

50

TO SOUTH LAKE TAHOE

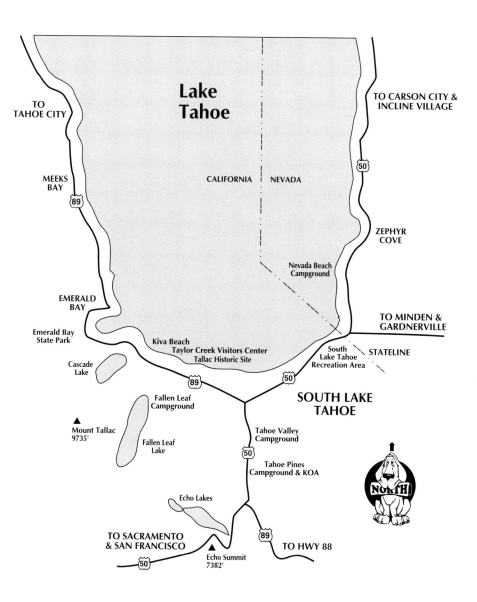

Lake Tahoe

TO TAHOE CITY

TO CARSON CITY & INCLINE VILLAGE

MEEKS BAY

89

50

CALIFORNIA | NEVADA

ZEPHYR COVE

Nevada Beach Campground

EMERALD BAY

TO MINDEN & GARDNERVILLE

Emerald Bay State Park

Kiva Beach
Taylor Creek Visitors Center
Tallac Historic Site

STATELINE

Cascade Lake

South Lake Tahoe Recreation Area

89

50

Fallen Leaf Campground

SOUTH LAKE TAHOE

▲ Mount Tallac 9735'

Fallen Leaf Lake

Tahoe Valley Campground

50

Tahoe Pines Campground & KOA

Echo Lakes

TO SACRAMENTO & SAN FRANCISCO

89

TO HWY 88

50

▲ Echo Summit 7382'

DOG RULES

1. The dog is not allowed in the house.

2. OK, the dog can come into the house, but only with certain rules.

3. The dog is allowed in all rooms, but has stay off the furniture.

4. The dog can get on the old furniture.

5. Fine. The dog is allowed on all furniture, but is not allowed to sleep with the humans on the bed.

6. OK, the dog is allowed to sleep on the bed, but by invitation only.

7. The dog can sleep on the bed whenever it wants but not under the covers.

8. The dog can sleep under the covers by invitation only.

9. The dog can sleep under the covers every night.

10. Humans must ask permission to sleep under the covers with the dog.

–Anonymous

TEN FAVORS A DOG ASKS OF MAN

1. My life lasts between 10 and 15 years. Every separation from you means suffering for me. Think about this before you decide whether or not to take me.

2. Give me time to understand what you are asking from me.

3. Instill confidence in me, I thrive on it.

4. Don't be angry with me for a long time, and don't lock me up for punishment. You have your work, your pleasure, your joy, I only have you.

5. Talk often to me. Even if I don't understand you completely, I do understand the tone of your voice when you talk to me.

6. Know that no matter how I am being treated, I shall never forget it.

7. Keep in mind before you hit me, that my jaws could crush the knuckles of your hand with ease, but that I don't make use of them.

8. Before scolding me when working with me, consider: perhaps I am uncomfortable from digesting my last meal; perhaps I was exposed to the sun too long; or perhaps I have a worn out heart.

9. Take care of me when I am old. You too, are born to be old one day.

10. Be with me when my going is rough. Everything is easier for me when you are beside me.

–Unknown

Alone Again

I wish someone would tell me what it is
   That I've done wrong.
Why I have to stay chained up and
   Left alone so long.
They seemed so glad to have me
   When I came here as a pup.
There were so many things we'd do
   While I was growing up.
They couldn't wait to train me as a
   Companion and a friend.
And told me how they'd never fear
   Being left alone again.
The children said they'd feed me and
   Brush me every day.
They'd play with me and walk me
   If only I could stay.
But now the family 'Hasn't time'
   They often say I shed.
They do not even want me in the house
   Not even to be fed.
The children never walk me.
   They always say "Not now!"
I wish that I could please them.
   Won't somebody tell me how?
All I had, you see, was love.
   I wish they would explain
Why they said they wanted me
   Then left me on a chain?

–Anonymous

The Rainbow Bridge

There is a bridge connecting Heaven and Earth. It is called the Rainbow Bridge because of its many colors. Just this side of the Rainbow Bridge is a land of meadows, hills and valleys, all of it covered with lush green grass.

When a beloved pet dies, the pet goes to this lovely land. There is always food and water and warm spring weather. There, the old and frail animals are young again. Those who are maimed are made whole once more. They play all day with each other, content and comfortable.

There is only one thing missing. They are not with the special person who loved them on Earth. So each day they run and play until the day comes when one suddenly stops playing and looks up! Then, the nose twitches! The ears are up! The eyes are staring! You have been seen, and that one suddenly runs from the group!

You take him or her in your arms and embrace. Your face is kissed again and again and again, and you look once more into the eyes of your trusting pet.

Then, together, you cross the Rainbow Bridge, never again to be separated.

—Unknown

Teddy, Springer Spaniel Pup

I wish people would realize
that animals are totally dependent,
helpless, like children;
a trust that is put upon us.

–James Herriot

THINGS WE CAN LEARN FROM A DOG

- Never pass up the opportunity to go for a joy ride.

- Allow the experience of fresh air and the wind in your face to be pure ecstasy.

- When loved ones come home, always run to greet them.

- When it's in your best interest, always practice obedience.

- Let others know when they've invaded your territory.

- Take naps and always stretch before rising.

- Run, romp and play daily.

- Eat with gusto and enthusiasm.

- Be loyal.

- Never pretend to be something you're not.

- If what you want lies buried, dig until you find it.

- When someone is having a bad day, be silent, sit close by and nuzzle them gently.

- Delight in the simple joy of a long walk.

- Thrive on attention and let people touch you.

- Avoid biting when a simple growl will do.

- On hot days, drink lots of water and lie under a shady tree.

- When you are happy, dance around and wag your entire body.

- No matter how often you are criticized, don't buy into the guilt thing and pout. Run right back and make friends.

–Unknown

A

Agate Bay Animal Hospital 95
Alder Inn 16
Alpine Animal Hospital 96, 99
Alpine Cafe 31
Alpine Fence Company 103
Alpine-Round Hill Animal Clinic 96
Alpine Village Motel 12
Ames Deli Mart 30
Angora Lakes 61, 67
Animal Works 94
Annual Pet Walk 89

B

Barker Pass 60
Bayer's Bagel Bakery 36
Beachside Inn & Suite 19
Bed & Breakfast for Pets 98
Best Western Lake Tahoe Inn 18
Beyond Obedience 102
Big Bend 64
Big Meadows Trail 53
Blackwood Canyon 60, 66, 75
Blue Jay Lodge 16
Blue Lake Motel 17
Blue Onion 31
Boca Reservior 81
Brockway Summit Sledding Hill 70

C

C & C Pet Stop 94
Cabin Creek Trail 64
Carr, Feely & Lindsey Lakes
        Trails 56
Cascade Falls Trail 47
CB's Pizza & Grill 31
Char Pit 31
Chris's Cafe 36

Coffee Connection 31
Coldwell Banker Hauserman
        Rental Group 12
Coldwell Banker Incline Realty 15
Colombo's Burgers A-Go-Go 36
Coon St. Beach 74
Cottonwood Campground 22
Coyotes Mexican Grill 32
Crag Lake 47

D

Dairy Queen 30
Dairy Queen Puppy Cup 86
Days Inn South Lake Tahoe 19
Desolation Wilderness Fishing 81
Diamond Peak Cross Country 66, 89
Diamond Peak Snow Play Area 71
Dog House and Cattery 94, 98
Dog Trainer, The 102
Doggie Day Care & Overnight
        Boarding 100
Donner Memorial State Park 22, 64
Donner Peak 42
Donner-Truckee Veterinary
        Hospital 95
Double Dawg Jawg 87
Dress Up Your Dog Contest 87

E

Eagle Lakes 43, 57
Eagle Falls Trail 47
Eagle Rock 46
East Shore Beaches 76
Echo Lakes 67, 77, 83
Echo Lakes Trail 50
Echo Lakes Boat Ride 90
Echo Summit Sno-Park 71
Ellis Peak Trail 45

Emerald Bay Boat-In Camp 25, 89
Emerald Bay State Park 25
Emerald Bay Veterinary Hospital 96
Emigrant Lake Trail 53

F
Falcon Lodge 13
Fallen Leaf Lake 77, 82
Fallen Leaf Lake Campground 26
Fallen Leaf Lake Trail 50
Family Tree Restaurants
        & Motel 13
Fast Eddies Texas Bar-B-Que 32
Fiamma Cucina Rustica 32
Fishing Charters 86, 91
Five Lakes Trail 44
Fountain Place Trail 52, 67
Four Paws Grooming and
        Boarding 98, 99
Freel Meadows Trail 52
Frog Point 43

G
Gateway Deli 30
Gateway Pets 94, 97
General Creek Mtn Biking 60
General Creek Campground 24
Glenshire Sledding Hill 70
Goose Meadows Campground 23
Granite Flat Campground 48
Granite Lake Trail 48
Grass Roots Natural Foods 36
Grass Lake Meadow 67
Grazie 32
Grog & Grist Market and Deli 35
Guy Yeaman 102

H
Hamburger Delite 35
Harrah's Tahoe 15
Hawley Grade Trail 49
High Country Lodge 16
High Sierra Pet Connection 100
Holiday House 12
Homeside Motel 15
Hurricane Beach 75

I
Incline Royal Pet Care 101
Incline Veterinary Hospital 96, 99
Incline Village Beach 75
Incline Village Sledding Hill 71
Invisible Fencing of Sierra 103
Izzy's Burger Spa 34, 36

J
J&J Pizza 37
Jacki Wright's Mobile Dog & Cat
        Grooming 98
Java Hut 33
Jen's In-Home Pet Care 100
Jo-Mar's Pet Coiffures 97
Joni's Cafe 33

K
Kaspian Campground 24
Karp's Pizza 37
Kentucky Fried Chicken 33, 37
Killer Chicken 37
Kingsbury Veterinary Hospital 96
Kirkwood BBQ & Campfire 91
Kiva Beach 76
KOA of South Lake Tahoe 26
Kokanee Salmon Festival 90

L

La Baer Inn 16
Lake Forest Campground
    & Beach 24, 74
Lake Margaret Trail 52, 61
Lake Tahoe Accommodations 15
Lake Tahoe Lodging 15
Lake Tours 86
Lakepark Lodge 16
Lakeview Pets 94
Loch Leven Lakes Trail 43
Logger Campground 22

M

Manzanita Motel 18
Marlette Lake Trail 61
Martis Creek Campground 22
Martis Creek Lake 74, 80
Martis Peak Trail 44, 59, 65
McKinney Rubicon Springs 66
Meeks Bay Campground 25
Meyers Downtown Cafe 37
Mickey's Pet Shop 94, 97
Montgomery Inn 16
Motel 6 18
Mount Watson Peak Trail 59
Mount Rose Campground 25
Mount Rose Trail 48
Mount Tallac 49
Mt. Lola 42, 57
Mr. Toad's Wild Ride 61
Mustard Seed 33

N

Naughty Dawg 33
Naughty Dawg Monster
    Dog Pull 87
Nevada Beach & Campground 27

Norfolk Woods Inn 14
North Lake Lodge 14
North Lake Veterinary
    Clinic 95, 97, 99
North Shore Lodge 13
North Tahoe Regional Park 65, 70

O

Obexer's Country Market 35
Ophir Creek Trail 49, 60

P

Pacific Crest Trail 42
Page Meadows 59, 65
Pampered Pet Care 100
Paws N Poseys 101
Peace of Mind Home Services 101
Perkins Pretty Good Kitchen 35
Petalk 102
Pet & Company 100, 101
Pet Nanny 101
Pet Pantry 95
Pet Shack 94, 97
Pet Sitting Plus 100
Paw Spa 98
Pet Supermarket 95
Pet World 95, 98
Port of Subs 30
Posh Paws 98
Prosser Creek Reservior 81

R

Rafting Down the Truckee 86
Ralston Peak Trail 51
Ravenwood Hotel 16
Red Carpet Inn 18
Reining Cats and Dogs 100

Rosie's Cafe 33
Rude Brothers Bagel & Coffee
    Haus 38
Rustic Cottages 13

S
Sagehen Creek 81
Sagehen Trail 64
Sandy Beach Campground 24
Scott's Delicatessen 38
Shirley Lake Trail 44
Sidestreet Cafe 38
Sierra Deli & Market 38
Sierra Mountain Doggie Camp 88
Sierra Pet Clinic of Truckee 95, 97
Sierra Veterinary Hospital 96, 99
Silver Creek Campground 23
Sizzler 30
Skunk Harbor 48
Sno-Park Permits 104
Snow Flake Drive In 38
South Lake Tahoe Rec Area 26
South Shore Cafe 38
South Shore Fence 103
South Tahoe Veterinary
    Hospital 96, 99
Spooner Lake 82
Spooner Summit Sledding Hill 71
Sprouts 38
Squaw Creek Trail 44
Squaw Valley Mtn Biking 58
Squaw Valley Tram Ride 86
Stampede Reservior 81
Starbucks Coffee 30
Stevenson's Inn 13
Subway 33, 36, 38
Super 8 Lodge 12
Summit Lake 43

Sun Dog Obedience 102
Sunnyside Market 35
Sunset Inn 12
Susie Lake 50
Syd's Bagelery & Espresso 34

T
T's Mesquite Rotisserie 36
Taco Bell 39
Taco Station 30
Tahoe City Sledding Hill 70
Tahoe Country Inn 16
Tahoe Fence Company 103
Tahoe Hidden Fencing 103
Tahoe House & Backerei 35
Tahoe Keys Delicatessen 39
Tahoe Lake Cottages 14
Tahoe Marina Inn 17
Tahoe Meadows 66, 70
Tahoe Pines Campground 27
Tahoe State Recreation Area 23, 74
Tahoe Valley Campground 26
Tahoe Valley Motel 18
Tahoma Lodge 14
Tallac Historic Site 77
Taylor Creek 83
Taylor Creek Sno-Park 67, 71
Taylor Creek Visitors Center 90
Ternullo's Creamery & Cafe 39
Thirsty Duck Bar & Grill 39, 91
Timberlake Inn 19
Todd Webb 102
Trade Winds Motel 18
Truckee River Access 23, 74, 80
Truckee-Sierra Boarding Kennel 98
Truckee Sledding Hill 70

V

Velma Lakes Trail 47

W

Ward Creek Canyon 45, 59
Watson Lake 75
Wedding Chapels 88, 91
West Shore Cafe 35
Western States Trail 58
Wild Cherries 31
Wilderness Permits 105
Wildflower Cafe 36
William B Layton Memorial Park 75
William Kent Campground 24
Wishing Well Espresso 34
Woodvista Lodge 13

Y

Yellow Submarine 39

Z

Zena's 31
Zephyr Cove Campground 27

NOTES

 NOTES